Better Homes and Gardens

TREASURY OF
CHRISTMAS
IDEAS

And a Selection of Favorite
Stories, Poems, and Carols

MEREDITH PRESS
New York   Des Moines

Acknowledgments

Many people have aided in one way or another in the production of the TREASURY of CHRISTMAS IDEAS. To these people we are deeply grateful.

To the designers, too numerous to name, we extend special thanks for letting us display their work and share their ideas with the Christmas decorators.

We are indebted to those who gave us permission to reprint the seasonal favorite stories, poems, and songs. Finally, the artists and photographers cannot be omitted. Their skill and talent are valuable and indispensible to the making of this Christmas volume.

The estate of Heywood Broun for "Inasmuch" by Heywood Broun. Reprinted by permission of Haywood Hale Broun and Constance M. Broun.

Grace Castagnetta for the Christmas carols arranged by Grace Castagnetta and Hendrik Willem Van Loon. Reprinted by permission of Grace Castagnetta.

The Macmillan Company for "All Through The Night" by Rachel Field. Copyright 1940, by The Macmillan Company. Renewed 1968, by Arthur S. Pederson. Reprinted by permission of The Macmillan Company.

Marianne Moore for "Rosemary" from THE COMPLETE POEMS OF MARIANNE MOORE. Copyright 1954, by Marianne Moore. Reprinted by permission of The Viking Press, Inc.

"A Song" by Phyllis McGinnely from MERRY CHRISTMAS, HAPPY NEW YEAR by Phyllis McGinnely. Copyright 1951 by Phyllis McGinnely. Reprinted by permission of The Viking Press, Inc.

Photographers: Horst Ahlberg, Edward Bourdon, Ernest Broun, George de Gennaro, Clark Dean, John Hartley, Thomas Hashimoto, Haycox Photoramics, Inc., Hedrich-Blessing, William Hopkins, Kranzten Studios, Vincent Lisanti, Dean Paris, George Peterson, John Rogers, Allen Snook, George Szanik, Fritz Taggart, Stanley Warren.

CONTENTS

6

His name was called Jesus

And it came to pass in those days, that there went out a decree from Caesar Augustus, that all the world should be taxed. (And this taxing was first made when Cyrenius was governor of Syria.) And all went to be taxed, every one into his own city.

And Joseph also went up from Galilee, out of the city of Nazareth, into Judaea, unto the city of David, which is called Bethlehem; (because he was of the house and lineage of David:) to be taxed with Mary his espoused wife, being great with child. And so it was, that, while they were there, the days were accomplished that she should be delivered. And she brought forth her first-born son, and wrapped him in swaddling clothes, and laid him in a manger; because there was no room for them in the inn.

And there was in the same country shepherds abiding in the field, keeping watch over their flock by night. And, lo, the angel of the Lord came upon them, and the glory of the Lord shone round about them: and they were sore afraid. And the angel said unto them, Fear not: for, behold, I bring you good tidings of great joy, which shall be to all people. For unto you is born this day in the city of David a Savior, which is Christ the Lord. And this shall be a sign unto you; Ye shall find the babe wrapped in swaddling clothes, lying in a manger. And suddenly there was with the angel a multitude of the heavenly hosts praising God, and saying, Glory to God in the highest, and on earth peace, good will toward men.

And it came to pass, as the angels were gone away from them into heaven, the shepherds said one to another, Let us now go even unto Bethlehem, and see this thing which is come to pass, which the Lord hath made known unto us. And they came with haste, and found Mary, and Joseph, and the babe lying in a manger. And when they had seen it, they made known abroad the saying which was told them concerning this child. And all they that heard it wondered at those things which were told them by the shepherds. But Mary kept all these things, and pondered them in her heart.

And the shepherds returned, glorifying and praising God for all the things that they had heard and seen, as it was told unto them. And when eight days were accomplished for the circumcising of the child, his name was called JESUS.

Luke 2:1-21

The Adoration of the Shepherds, Giorgione National Gallery of Art, Washington, D. C. Samuel H. Kress Collection.

La Befana

An Italian Christmas Legend

It is a great mistake to think that there are no fairies in Italy, and one of the nicest is called La Befana, and she belongs to Christmas just like the holly and mistletoe and snowmen. She comes only once a year as the Three Kings do for the Epiphany, and she is not young and beautiful, but old and bent and almost more like a witch than a fairy. In fact before people realized how kind she was, they thought of her as a wicked witch and rang bells made of earthenware and blew glass trumpets on the evening of the fifth of January on purpose to frighten her away; children were even taught incantations to save them from her power. But all this has been forgotten now, and anyhow, the Befana never deserved it as her story will show.

The first thing to notice about her is that she is very ancient, and when Our Lord was born the Befana was already a little bent and her hair was white. She had a tiny cottage outside Bethlehem and after her old husband died she lived there alone, and she was always rather sad because she had no children to keep her company.

Well it happened that the winter two thousand years ago was extremely cold and all the poor people suffered very much, and the Befana got so stiff in the knees that she couldn't hurry for anyone, but still, when her store of firewood got low, she had to struggle out into a little wood at hand on the opposite hill to where her cottage stood; but on that particular night the moonlight was so wonderful that the Befana could hardly tear herself away from the window, and if she had known how to read she could easily have done so without a candle. Somehow the whole world seemed alive; "Why, how strange," thought the Befana, "the sky looks as though it were quivering; I'm sure I see things moving, and what a frost there must be, I can hear the ground singing." And though she was not at all an imaginative person, she stayed at the window a long time, and it was past midnight when she went to bed. She woke up late and the sun was shining and the air was very crisp and brilliant, and the Befana felt very elated and hardly groaned at all about her old bones though she was stiffer than ever and there wasn't much in the pot for dinner. Still there it was, she felt so unaccountably happy that she began to sing even while she lit the fire and cooked.

A few days passed and then one afternoon she went out to gather some sticks and it took her rather longer than usual, so by the time she had brought down one bundle the sun was beginning to set and an unusually bright star shone in the sky. She was just starting to go and fetch the other two bundles she had left a little way up the hill when a party of riders drew up at her gate. There were quite a lot of them and they had evidently come a long journey for there were camels and mules laden with baggage and a number of servants dressed in a strange outlandish fashion, not at all like what one saw around Bethlehem. The Befana stared hard at them and she noticed that some of them had dark faces and she heard them chattering in an unknown tongue. Toward the end of the procession came three men riding together on camels, and when they saw the Befana they stopped and one of them, a very dignified old man with a long white beard, called to her with rather a foreign accent: "My good woman would you tell us whether the city yonder be Bethlehem?"

"Surely it is, sir," answered the Befana, "but I doubt if you will find any lodging there; every corner is full to overflowing with folk come for the census and fine grumbling one hears at these new laws made just to disturb honest working men and take them from their homes in the middle of winter. But they do say too how Master Matthew, the inn keeper, has made a fortune by charging whatever he liked just for a roof and shelter, and Matthew was always fond of money. You are late though, if you have come for the census, for the last day of enrollment is tomorrow and the officials complain that they are worked to death."

"We are not come to enroll ourselves," answered the old man, "for we are from a far off land not subject to Caesar. God the Almighty One has put it into our hearts to seek for His Christ, the great King of the Jews, who is now newly born, and He has sent that most bright star to guide us to where we may find and worship Him, and I think we are near to our journey's end. How is it that you have heard nought of this matter?"

The Befana listened in round-eyed amazement, even she could see that these were no ordinary travelers, and there was the star shining as no other star ever shone; it all sounded very wonderful, and almost before she knew what she was saying she had cried out: "Oh sir, couldn't I find that King too?"

"Certainly," replied the old man, "but you must come with us at once for we cannot dally by the way since our star never stops." And he made as though to go on.

"Oh sir, sir, do wait a moment; just a little half hour while I go and fetch the bundles of wood I have left out on the hill; if I don't go and get them now that rascal John, the wood-man, will surely steal them and then where should I be! But I will be very quick."

So the Befana hobbled hurriedly away only just to fetch her bundles of sticks, but the old man shook his head and pointing to the star he gave the signal to move on and when the poor old Befana came back the caravan had disappeared; she thought she could still hear the camel bells tinkling in the distance.

"Oh dear, oh dear," cried the Befana, "whatever shall I do now? They have left me behind, but I suppose I ought not to have thought such fine quality as themselves could wait for an old woman like me. How shall I ever find Christ that King?"

Then quite suddenly the Befana found herself wringing her hands and crying and not caring for anything, not even for the bundles of wood nor her supper; she only wanted to follow the riders. She began to run along the road and then such an extraordinary thing happened; she found she was running faster and faster, and she didn't feel old any longer, only the city seemed so far away she despaired of ever getting there.

The first person she met was a peasant, and she stopped rather out of breath. "Tell me," she panted, "have you seen a party of riders pass this way? I have missed them and must catch them up."

"A party of riders, did you say?" answered the peasant slowly. "Yes, I saw them and they spoke to me and I told them what I could. We don't often see such folk in these parts but their coming must be all part of the strange happenings of these last days."

"What happenings do you mean?" asked the Befana. "My cottage is too far from the village and now I am old and can't move much so I hear but little news."

"What," returned the peasant, "you don't mean to say you have not heard what befell the shepherds out on the hill some twelve nights ago? Why my own cousin was among them, and

wonderful it was and fearful too, for they saw first one angel who appeared quite close to them and talked with them as man to man, and told them of a newborn Saviour who is indeed to be the king of our own poor country and of all the world. And the angel told them to hurry over the hill, that hill opposite to your own cottage, to a cave that all the shepherds know of, and there they would find the Child newborn and lying in a manger. And my cousin says that then all of a sudden he and the other shepherds felt themselves surrounded by a host of angelic beings, and the sky was filled with forms of light and they heard music most sweet and marvelous and words of peace and praise. And all their fear left them, the dogs began to bark, the sheep to bleat and the lambs to frolic, and he and his fellows ran quickly over the hill until they came to the cave. A man was watching at the entrance but he let them pass and there they found a woman, young and very fair, gazing at a newborn Babe who was lying in a manger while an ox and ass breathed gently on him as though to warm him, and the cave was filled with light and the sound of heavenly singing.

"Then the shepherds were seized with joy unspeakable, though they durst speak to no one there, and when they came away they had to sing too for the great gladness that filled their hearts. At first they wondered that the Child should be found thus in a cave, but it seems that Master Matthew had refused the man and woman lodging in the inn, they having no money to pay and being poor people like ourselves. I tell you, my cousin is a changed man from all this and he came to tell us of these marvels, but it is not good to speak of them openly for some men jeer and call us poor deluded fools, and others might be minded to do that child some harm. But I have told you because the Old Wise Man, whom I take to be a King, warned me that perchance a woman would follow in their steps and he charged me to entreat you never to give up the search until you, too, have found the Child and His Mother. And even I, who am only a poor peasant, have seen them, not indeed in the cave but in an humble dwelling on the outskirts of the city where they had found shelter; and though I saw no light nor heard any singing, all that mattered little, for when you find that Child I think you find the greatest good in the whole world. And now you must go on, and if you are ready to follow the guiding of the Star which is the desire of your own heart, you will surely find him too; but you look to me young, not old, and I think you still have a long way

to go.'' And with this he turned away.

The Befana listened to all the peasant had said, and she thought bitterly of how she might already have found Him and how she had missed her opportunity just by being so anxious about those faggots. What did she care for them now, neither they, nor her house, nor anything mattered at all, only the burning desire of her heart of which the peasant had spoken.

So she went on stopping at many houses to ask if here was the Babe, the King of the Jews, and the boys threw mud at her, while their parents laughed and mocked and others threatened to have her locked up as a mad woman, or a political agitator talking so dangerously of new kings, and she could find no house sheltering a man and woman and newborn babe. Even when she asked for news of a caravan of riders, she only heard that they had indeed been seen but were gone on their way again, no one knew where. So very sad and extremely tired, the Befana sank down under an archway and fell asleep, and while she slept she dreamed of the Old Man who had spoken to her, of all the peasant had told her, and in the far distance she seemed to see a child beckoning to her and she woke just as she was starting to run toward him.

And so the Befana's long journey began, and at first it took her all over the earth and into every corner of the world; she crossed the great mountain ranges, and deserts and oceans; she forded rivers and passed through forests. And so she saw all the beauty God had created, and met many strange animals, and she found that they too knew of the Baby King for the ox and ass had spread the story abroad, very pleased with themselves for the part they had played; and not to be outdone the sheep had told, too, of how they had heard the angels' song on the hill; but though the beasts all directed the Befana as best they could, she did not find their advice of much use. As to men, she soon gave up asking them anything for they only contradicted each other, but she thought that if she went quite steadily to every child, in the end she was bound to find that one baby for whom she was searching. And remembering the Kings and their long caravan of pack mules laden with gifts, she got an old sack and filled it with every kind of thing that children most enjoy; only I think there must have been something magical about that sack, for though the Befana is still traveling, it never gets too heavy or full for her to carry, and yet she never gets to the bottom or runs short of toys.

Gradually Italy came to be her special country for further north she found Saint Nicholas was busy looking after children's Christmas presents, and he called himself Santa Claus

and dressed up like a grandfather snowman for the occasion; and though he was a saint, he was very annoyed when he found the Befana who was reputed to be a witch trespassing on his ground, so he promptly sent her away, promising that when he found the Christ Child he would let her know, but this he only said to get rid of her. However Saint Nicholas had so much to do in his own country that he never got to Italy, so there the Befana had the field all to herself, and every year just after Christmas she goes the rounds of the children from the Alps to Sicily, slipping into their nurseries when they are asleep and she always leaves them a present. Only if they have been naughty, then she leaves a little bit of coal too just to show that she knows all about their misdemeanors.

And isn't it a proof of how stupid men can be, that in spite of the Befana's obvious good will, they should ever have thought her to be a wicked witch and threatened children that she would come and carry them off as though she had been the boogeyman. Now I am glad to say, people have grown wiser and little boys no longer sing rude songs about her, and the earthenware bells and glass trumpets that used to be made to frighten her away have all been forgotten.

But still the Befana prefers that no one shall see her, so it is useless for children to pinch themselves to keep awake on the night when she is expected, and of course being a fairy she has every right to be invisible whenever she chooses. Very often too she lets other people give the presents for her but you may be sure that, though she can't be seen, she is there all the time smiling in the corner.

Naturally in all this long time the Befana has gotten to know any number of children for she goes into palaces where the King's little sons and daughters hang out their stockings just like the children of the gardener or the chimney sweep, but I think she has always found the kings of the earth very different from the Baby who was King in Bethlehem. That is why she really feels more at home among the poor, and the poorer the parents, the more presents the Befana would like to leave for the children, for she feels like a mother to them all. And if she meets some who have no homes and no stocking to hang up, why then she can't rest till she sees they have what they want. If the Befana could have her way, every poor child would be taken out of the streets and the towns and set down in a nice clean cottage surrounded with fields full of flowers and little scurrying rabbits, and every flower would have the magic gift of making the child who picked it perfectly happy. But

search as she may among the poorest people of town or country, she has never found anyone as poor as that man and woman in the hillside cave, and never a baby cradled in a manger with an ox and ass to warm him.

Sometimes when that Baby seemed further off than ever, the Befana even thought of looking for Him in the Presepi, the Christmas Cribs which are set up in the churches, and once she managed to get into the great church in Rome where at Midnight Mass on Christmas Eve is shown the cradle of Our Lord. "Now surely at last," thought the Befana, "I shall see the Bambino Gesu;" she prayed so hard and scarcely dared to look up, so much did she long to see a little living Child lying in the cradle, but though the choir sang most sweetly, it was not the song of the angels, and when, at last through the mist of incense and many lights she did look at the altar, she saw the cradle was empty.

It was the same with the other Presepi all over the country, and really very often the Befana hardly knew whether to laugh or cry to see how mistaken the people were who had the making of them. She would have liked to arrange one herself, but that couldn't be, for even good fairies are not allowed to go interfering with the handiwork of pious friars. In some of the Presepi indeed there were all kinds of strange folk whom the Befana did not even know, for though the shepherds and the Kings had their old place nearest to the manger, there were masons, carpenters, milkmaids, and buxom housewives, fine ladies and cavaliers grouped about in the landscape, all the world and his wife seemed to be there. She was not much interested in them for they were all of them outsiders, come since her Bethlehem days; but even when she recognized her friends, the Kings and the peasant with his cousin the shepherd, she couldn't help noticing how very smart they had become; even the shepherds had discarded the thick cloaks they used to wear on the hills in cold December nights, while the Kings had crowns on their heads and robes of crimson and ermine, whereas there was she, the Befana, still in her travel-stained old clothes and rather ragged at that. And though she knew quite well that the figures in the Presepio were only dolls, nevertheless she envied them for they represented men and women who had found the Christ Child. They were all so smiling and happy. Had they, she wondered, found Him then so easily without any trouble or long search? Oh, if only she had not bothered about those wretched faggots she might have been there too, and the Befana

felt she would willingly do the humblest work, carrying sticks all day long if need be, if only she might stand every year in her appointed place near the Kings and see the Child and His Mother smiling on her too. And the poor old Befana sank down on the step of a chapel and began to cry. She stayed there quite a long time never noticing the people as they came and went, or the children as they jostled past her in their anxiety to get a good view of the Presepio. When she looked up again the church was empty. She thought she heard a titter, and lo and behold, all the figures in the Presepio were laughing, but laughing so kindly that she didn't feel a bit hurt, and the old King beckoned her to approach. Then the man who was nearest to the Mother and Child, he whom the shepherds had seen watching the entrance to the cave, turned toward her. "Poor old Befana," he said, "you have been searching for a very long while but you are just a little mistaken. You want to find the Bambino Gesu as He was that night in Bethlehem when the angels sang in the sky, but that cannot be. The Christ Child cannot now be found in one human child, but in all children; He is in each one to whom you give your gifts for the One dwells in the many, and the searching never ends nor does the finding. Your place is not here, but among all living children." And the laughter ceased, Saint Joseph and the King fell back into their fixed positions and the Befana hurried away quite happily for she remembered how many children were still waiting for her.

Now I think this episode happened to the Befana about two hundred years ago and though I have no documents to prove it is true; things often happen in the lives of fairies that never get into the official biographies. In some Presepi, moreover, of about that time you may even see in one corner among all the other folk, a nice tidy old woman with a tall hat rather like a witch's and a bundle of sticks in her apron, and a chance acquaintance might easily take her for the Befana.

But I am sure that after what Saint Joseph said, the Befana doesn't really want a place among the dolls; she is much too alive and busy for that, and now that she knows the searching and finding go together, she is quite happy.

And so this is a story that can't have any proper ending, for there will be Christmas and children as long as the world lasts, and if our dear old ragged Befana deserted us now, we should have to hunt out all our former bells and glass trumpets, only this time they would be used to call her back.

The Mouse That Didn't Believe in Santa Claus

by Eugene Field

The clock stood, of course, in the corner; a moonbeam floated idly on the floor, and a little mauve mouse came from the hole in the chimney corner and frisked and scampered in the light of the moonbeam upon the floor. The little mauve mouse was particularly merry; sometimes she danced upon two legs and sometimes upon four legs, but always very daintily and always very merrily.

"Ah, me," sighed the old clock, "how different mice are nowadays from the mice we used to have in the old times! Now there was your grandma, Mistress Velvetpaw, and there was your grandpa, Master Sniffwhisker—how grave and dignified they were! Many a night have I seen them dancing upon the carpet below me, but always that stately minuet and never that crazy frisking which you are executing now, to my surprise—yes, and to my horror, too!"

"But why shouldn't I be merry?" asked the little mauve mouse. "Tomorrow is Christmas, and this is Christmas Eve."

"So it is," said the old clock. "I had really forgotten all about it. But, tell me, what is Christmas to you, little Miss Mauve Mouse?"

"A great deal to me!" cried the little mauve mouse. "I have been very good for a very long time; I have not used any bad words, nor have I gnawed any holes, nor have I stolen any canary seed, nor have I worried my mother by running behind the flour barrel where that horrid trap is set. In fact, I have been so good that I'm very sure Santa Claus will bring me something very pretty."

This seemed to amuse the old clock mightily; in fact, the old clock fell to laughing so heartily that in an unguarded moment she struck twelve instead of ten, which was exceedingly careless.

"Why, you silly little mauve mouse," said the old clock, "you don't believe in Santa Claus, do you?"

"Of course I do," answered the mauve mouse. "Believe in Santa Claus? Why shouldn't I? Didn't Santa Claus bring me a beautiful butter

cracker last Christmas, and a lovely gingersnap, and a delicious rind of cheese, and—lots of things? I should be very ungrateful if I did *not* believe in Santa Claus, and I certainly shall not disbelieve in him at the very moment when I am expecting him to arrive with a bundle of goodies for me.

"I once had a little sister," continued the little mauve mouse, "who did not believe in Santa Claus, and the very thought of the fate that befell her makes my blood run cold and my whiskers stand on end. She died before I was born, but my mother has told me all about her. Her name was Squeaknibble, and she was in stature one of those long, low, rangy mice that are seldom found in well-stocked pantries. Mother says that Squeaknibble took after our ancestors who came from England, and seemed to inherit many ancestral traits, the most conspicuous of which was a disposition to sneer at some of the most respected dogmas in mousedom. From her very infancy she doubted, for example, the widely accepted theory that the moon was composed of green cheese; and this heresy was the first intimation her parents had of her skeptical turn of mind. Of course, her parents were vastly annoyed, for they saw that this youthful skepticism would lead to serious, if not fatal, consequences. Yet all in vain did they reason and plead with their headstrong and heretical child.

"For a long time Squeaknibble would not believe that there was any such archfiend as a cat; but she came to be convinced one memorable night, on which occasion she lost two inches of her beautiful tail, and received so terrible a fright that for fully an hour afterward her little heart beat so violently as to lift her off her feet and bump her head against the top of our domestic hole. The cat that deprived my sister of so large a percentage of her tail was the same ogress that nowadays steals into this room, crouches treacherously behind the sofa, and feigns to be asleep, hoping, forsooth, that some of us, heedless of her hated presence, will venture within reach of her claws. So enraged was this ferocious monster at the escape of my sister that she ground her fangs viciously together, and vowed to take no pleasure in life until she held in her devouring jaws the innocent little mouse which belonged to the mangled bit of tail she even then clutched in her remorseless claws."

"Yes," said the old clock, "now that you recall the incident, I recollect it well. I was here then, and I remember that I laughed at the cat and chided her for her awkwardness. My reproaches irritated her; she told me that a clock's duty was to run itself down, *not* to be depreciating the merits of others! Yes, I recall the time; that cat's tongue is fully as sharp as her claws."

"Be that as it may," said the little mauve mouse, "it is a matter of history, and therefore beyond dispute, that from that very moment the cat pined for Squeaknibble's life; it seemed as if that one little two-inch taste of Squeaknibble's tail had filled the cat with a consuming appetite for the rest of Squeaknibble. So the cat waited and watched and hunted and schemed and devised and did everything possible for a cat—a cruel cat—to do in order to gain her murderous ends.

"One night—one fatal Christmas Eve—our mother had undressed the children for bed, and was urging upon them to go to sleep earlier than usual, since she fully expected that Santa Claus would bring each of them something very nice before morning. Thereupon the little dears whisked their cunning tails, pricked up their beautiful ears, and began telling one another what they hoped Santa Claus would bring. One asked for a slice of Roquefort, another for Swiss, another for Brick, and a fourth for Edam; one expressed a preference for Cream cheese, while another hoped for Camembert. There were four-teen little ones then, and consequently there were diverse opinions as to the kind of gift which Santa Claus should best bring; still there was, as you can readily understand, an enthusiastic agreement upon this point, namely, that the gift should be cheese of some brand or other.

" 'My dears,' said our mother, 'we should be content with whatsoever Santa Claus bestows, so long as it is cheese, disjoined from all traps whatsoever, unmixed with Paris green, and free from glass, strychnine, and other harmful ingre-dients. As for myself, I shall be satisfied with a cut of nice, fresh American cheese. So run away to your dreams now, that Santa may find you sleeping.'

"The children obeyed—all but Squeaknibble. 'Let the others think what they please,' said she, 'but I don't believe in Santa Claus. I'm not go-ing to bed, either. I'm going to creep out of this dark hole and have a quiet romp, all by myself, in the moonlight.' Oh, what a vain, foolish, wicked little mouse was Squeaknibble! But I will not reproach the dead; her punishment came all too swiftly. Now listen: who do you suppose over-heard her talking so disrespectfully of Santa Claus?"

"Why, Santa Claus himself," said the old clock.

"Oh, no," answered the little mauve mouse. "It was that wicked, murderous cat! Just as Satan lurks and lies in wait for naughty little mice. And you can depend upon it that, when that awful cat heard Squeaknibble speak so dis-respectfully of Santa Claus, her wicked eyes glowed with joy, her sharp teeth watered, and her bristling fur emitted electric sparks as big as peas. Then what did that bloody monster do but scuttle as fast as she could into Dear-my-Soul's room, leap up into Dear-my-Soul's crib, and walk off with the pretty little white muff which Dear-my-Soul used to wear when she went for a visit to the little girl in the next block! What upon earth did the horrid old cat want with Dear-my-Soul's pretty little white muff? Ah, the ingenuity of that cat! Listen.

"In the first place," resumed the little mauve mouse, after a pause that showed the depth of her emotion, "in the first place, that wretched cat dressed herself up in that pretty little white muff, by which you are to understand that she crawled through the muff just so far as to leave her four cruel legs at liberty."

"Yes, I understand," said the old clock.

"Then she put on the boy doll's cap," said the little mauve mouse, "and when she was arrayed in the boy doll's fur cap and Dear-my-Soul's pretty little white muff, of course she didn't look like a cruel cat at all. But whom did she look like?"

"Like the boy doll," suggested the old clock.

"No, no!" cried the little mauve mouse.

"Like Dear-my-Soul?" asked the old clock.

"How stupid you are!" exclaimed the little mauve mouse. "Why, she looked like Santa Claus, of course!"

"Oh, yes; I see," said the old clock. "Now I begin to be interested; go on."

"Alas!" sighed the little mauve mouse, "not much remains to be told; but there is more of my story left than there was of Squeaknibble when that horrid cat crawled out of that miserable disguise. You are to understand that, contrary to her mother's warning, Squeaknibble issued from the friendly hole in the chimney corner, and gamboled about over this very carpet, and, I dare say, in this very moonlight.

"Right merrily was Squeaknibble gamboling," continued the little mauve mouse, "and she had just turned a double somersault without the use of what remained of her tail, when, all of a sudden, she beheld, looming up like a monster ghost, a figure all in white fur! Oh, how frightened she was, and how her little heart did beat! 'Purr, pur-r-r,' said the ghost in white fur. 'Oh, please don't hurt me!' pleaded Squeaknibble. 'No; I'll not hurt you,' said the ghost in white fur; 'I'm Santa Claus, and I've brought you a beautiful piece of savory old cheese, you dear little mousie, you.' Poor Squeaknibble was deceived; a skeptic all her life, she was at last befooled by the most fatal of frauds. 'How good of you!' said Squeaknibble. 'I didn't believe there was a Santa Claus, and—' but before she could say more she was seized by two sharp, cruel claws that conveyed her crushed body to the murderous mouth of the cat. I can dwell no longer upon this harrowing scene. Before the morrow's sun rose upon the spot where that tragedy had been enacted, poor Squeaknibble passed to that bourne to which two inches of her beautiful tail had preceded her by the space of three weeks to a day. As for Santa Claus, when he came that Christmas Eve, bringing cheese and goodies for the other little mice, he heard with sorrow of Squeaknibble's fate; and ere he departed he said that in all his experience he had never known of a mouse or a child that had prospered after once saying he didn't believe in Santa Claus."

All Through the Night

By Rachel Field

All that day the Inn Yard had been thronged with people coming to pay their taxes in the town of Bethlehem. The small sturdy watchdog who slept in the stable and picked up what food he could find had never before seen such a crowd of travelers.

When night fell he was tired from barking at so many strangers and their beasts, and with scurrying out of the way of feet and hoofs. But for all the barking and running about it had been a good day. The Inn had overflowed into the yard. There had been a fire there with meat roasting over it and pots that sent out clouds of savory steam. Many a rich morsel had fallen his way, so he felt well content as he crept into his corner of the stable near the oxen's stall.

He and they greeted each other and exchanged news of the day.

"Yes, we too have been busy," the oxen told him. "Heavy loads for us since daybreak and the roads round Bethlehem so choked with carts and caravans and herds and flocks we could hardly move sometimes."

"And rude, stupid creatures they were to meet!" the ass put in from her corner. "With no manners at all or sense enough to follow their own noses. Some even dared to dispute the right of way with me, but I held my ground."

"I have no doubt you did," said the dog, for he knew the ass was not one to be persuaded against her will. He turned himself round and round in a pile of straw to make himself comfortable and fell to licking a bruised spot on his leg.

"There must have been many sheep," the old ewe joined in from her pen. "I could not see them because I was shut in here with my two lambs, but I could tell by their voices that some came from places farther away than Judea. I should have liked to see them."

"Well," the dog told her, "I found them a dusty, frightened lot. I was thankful not to have their herding in my charge. And the goats were no better," he added, that the bearded gray goat might be sure to hear. He and the goat were not upon friendly terms and took pleasure in tormenting each other.

"Peace and quiet. Peace and quiet at last," the doves cooed from the rafters. "Peace and quiet till morning, that is all we ask."

The hens made soft clucking sounds to show that they were in complete agreement.

But the cock with his scarlet comb and burnished tail feathers, stepping about in search of stray kernels, was of a different mind. "I like noise and bustle myself." He voiced his opinion loudly. "Peace is all very well for those who haven't the spirit for something better. Now *I* can hardly wait for morning."

"Everyone to his own taste," the mild-eyed cow put in her word, shifting her cud deftly and flicking her tail as she did so. "If it were always day or always night we should not all be satisfied."

"Well said. Well said," the doves agreed in drowsy unison from the dimness of the eaves.

Darkness gathered there first. The swallows were already seeking their nests, while the bats were beginning to stretch and unfold their lean, black wings.

Night was coming fast and all the birds and beasts and insects of the stable knew that it belonged to them. The world was theirs as the world of day could never be. When the sun rose man would be their master again. They would carry his burdens or feed or serve him according to their different gifts. But night was their own, when they might move or fight or take counsel together without man's interference. It was good that this should be so, the little dog thought, as he burrowed deeper into the straw.

His sworn enemy the cat slid by. She moved like a shadow with fiery-green eyes ready to pounce upon the mice who were already squeaking and scampering at their play. But the dog was too tired and comfortable to give chase, so for once he let her pass unmolested. All about him crickets chirped in rusty chorus and sometimes a bat swooped so low he could feel the stir of its wings. The darkness was warm and alive with the familiar scents of fur and feathers and grain and straw.

"Rest well. Rest well. Rest well." The doves cooed sleepily, making a soft sound in their throats that was like the bubbling of a well-filled pot over a fire.

Night had come to Bethlehem. The Inn had been full hours ago. The dog could hear late travelers being turned away. The stable door was securely bolted against intruders and the wind was rising, frosty and keen. Through an opening in the roof a star shone bright as purest silver.

"I never saw a star look so large or so near," the cock observed as he moved about with his spurred, high-stepping walk. "Somehow it makes me very restless, and there is something strange in the air. Perhaps you have felt it, too?"

But the dog made no answer. He yawned and laid his pointed muzzle on his paws and prepared himself for sleep.

He woke at the sound of voices outside and roused himself to bark. But though the hair rose along his back, no sound came rumbling from his throat. The bolt was drawn and the stable door opened to lantern light and the dim shapes of two men and a donkey on whose back a woman sat, wrapped in a heavy cloak.

"Well"—the voice of the Inn Keeper sounded short and impatient—"if you cannot go on, there is only the stable to offer. Coming as you have at such an hour, you are fortunate to have this shelter till morning."

"The roads were crowded," the Man answered him, "and our pace was slow because of my wife. You can see that she is nearly spent."

"Yes, yes." The Inn Keeper was already shutting the door. "I am sorry for your plight, but I tell you there is no room left."

The dog was on his feet. He could hear the other animals rising about him, yet not one of them uttered a sound. Their throats were as silent as his own.

In the flickering lantern light he watched the Man lift the Woman from the donkey's back and set her upon her feet. She was so weary she would have fallen but for the Man's arms.

"Joseph," she said, "you must not be troubled for me, even if it should be that the time has come." . . . She rested her head on the Man's shoulder and sighed so softly it might have been one of the doves in the rafters drawing closer to her mate.

"But, Mary," the Man went on, "it is not right and fitting that it should be here—not in a stable among the beasts."

"Who knows," she comforted him, "what is to be? These beasts are more kind than men who kill and hurt one another. I am glad to be here. Their warm breath comforts me. Their straw is clean and soft to rest upon."

Everywhere beyond the ring of light that the lantern made, bright eyes were upon the strangers. Furry eyes and quivering noses pointed,

alert and watchful.

The strange donkey, freed of his load, found a place beside the ass. He sank down, too tired to drink water from the trough or reach for a mouthful of hay.

A hush was on the stable. Not only were all throats silent, but no wings stirred; no claws scratched and not a hoof pounded. And in that hour nothing died. The young swallows and mice were safe from their enemies, for a mystery greater than death held them all in its power.

The lantern flickered and went out.

"Our oil is gone!" the Man cried out in distress.

"There will be light enough." The Woman spoke in a faint voice, and as if in answer the star in the roof gap shone brighter than before.

How long it was after that the little dog could not tell. Morning was still far off, yet the cock suddenly lifted up his voice, so shrill and clear it seemed he would split himself in two. It was not like any other cockcrow since the world began and it rose higher than the rafters and mounted to heaven itself. At the same instant each creature found voice and joined with him. Every living thing in the stable had a part in that swelling chorus of praise. Even the bees hummed till their hive throbbed with music, sweeter than all its store of honey.

"What manner of place is this?" the Man cried out. "What beasts are these who have the tongues of angels?"

But the Woman answered him softly out of the shadows. "It was they who gave us shelter this night. Let them draw near and be the first to worship."

She drew aside the folds of her cloak and light filled the stable even to the farthest corners. The dog cowered before such strange brightness. When he dared to look more closely he saw that it encircled the head of an infant, newborn.

"There is no bed for him to lie upon," the Man sighed. "Only this"—and he pointed to the manger.

"Bring it here," the Mother said. "My heart tells me there will be nights when he will have no place at all to rest his head."

So the Child lay quiet in the strawfilled wooden manger and all the animals came to view him there—the oxen, the cow, the ass and the donkey, the ewe and her lambs, the gray goat, the dog, the hens and the proud cock ruffling his feathers. The cat left off her prowling to join them and the mice ran beside her without fear. The crickets came, too, drawn from the comfort of their warm straw; the bees, from their snug hive. The tireless ants and spiders left their toil to draw near. The swallows in the eaves flew down; the bats bent low on their dark wings, and the doves came closest of all with their soft murmurs above the manger. When they had all seen the Wonder they returned to their places and were quiet again.

All but the dog. He could not rest as he had

before. He stretched himself beside the manger and lay with his head on his folded paws, his eyes wide and watchful as the hours passed.

Long before sunrise the door opened without sound of bolt being drawn and a band of Shepherds came in. They bore a strange tale on their lips and they also worshiped on bended knees. One carried a lamb in his arms and the Child answered its bleating with a smile.

"Behold the Lamb of God," they said one to another as they turned to go back to their flocks on the hills.

The star grew pale and through the gap in the stable roof morning showed rosy in the east. Even before the cock hailed it, the dog knew that the sun was up. But he did not move lest he rouse the three in his care. It was then that he saw a strange thing.

The rafters high above cast their shadows as the rising sun struck through. Two of the beams crossed in sharp black bars that fell directly across the sleeping Child. The little dog could not tell why the sight should make him cower in sudden fear.

Then the cock crowed three times and the first sounds of people stirring in the Inn and yard began.

He watched the Man and the Woman preparing to go. He saw the donkey being watered and fed and the blanket fitted in place. He saw the Mother wrap her Son warmly against the cold before the Man set them upon the donkey's back and lifted a heavy bundle on his own.

"Come," he said and opened the stable door. "We must make haste."

Stiff from his long vigil, the dog rose and followed them to the door. He watched them cross the Inn yard in the early light and join other travelers who were already thronging the roads leading to and from Bethlehem. Soon they would be lost to his sight, those Three whom he had guarded through the hours of darkness.

"Ah," cried the cock, preening his burnished feathers, "what a morning!" He strutted over to where bits of food and grain lay scattered and began to forage for stray morsels.

The dog lifted his head and sniffed hungrily. He could tell that pots were already on the fires. The sharp morning air brought the savory news to him and he knew that by keeping close to the kitchen he would soon be well filled. He remembered a bone he had buried yesterday in a secluded spot. Yet he did not seek it. He trotted past the kitchen doors, and though his nose twitched at the smells that he was leaving he kept it pointed straight ahead.

"Wait. Wait." His bark rang out sharp and determined and his paws clicked over the stones as he ran.

He did not pause till he had caught up with the Man who led the plodding donkey and his burden along the dusty road.

"Here I am!" He barked again as he fell into step beside them. "Let me come with you."

Inasmuch

By Heywood Broun

Once there lived near Bethlehem a man named Simon and his wife Deborah. And Deborah dreamed a curious dream, a dream so vivid that it might better be called a vision. It was not yet daybreak, but she roused her husband and told him that an angel had come to her in the vision and had said, as she remembered it, "Tomorrow night in Bethlehem the King of the World will be born." The rest was not so vivid in Deborah's mind, but she told Simon that wise men and kings were already on their way to Bethlehem, bringing gifts for the wonder child.

"When he is born," she said, "the wise men and the kings who bring these gifts will see the stars dance in the heavens and hear the voices of angels. You and I must send presents, too, for this child will be the greatest man in all the world."

Simon objected that there was nothing of value in the house to take to such a child, but Deborah replied, "The King of the World will understand." Then, although it was not yet light, she got up and began to bake a cake, and Simon went beyond the town to the hills and got holly and made a wreath. Later in the day husband and wife looked over all their belongings, but the only suitable gift they could find was one old toy, a somewhat battered wooden duck that had belonged to their eldest son, who had grown up and married and gone away to live in Galilee. Simon painted the toy duck as well as he could, and Deborah told him to take it and the cake and the wreath of holly and go to Bethlehem. "It's not much," she said, "but the King will understand."

It was almost sunset when Simon started down the winding road that led to Bethlehem. Deborah watched him round the first turn and would have watched longer except that he was walking straight toward the sun and the light hurt her eyes. She went back into the house and an hour had hardly passed when she heard Simon whistling in the garden. He was walking very slowly. At the door he hesitated for almost a minute. She looked up when he came in. He was empty handed.

"You haven't been to Bethlehem," said Deborah.

"No," said Simon.

"Then, where is the cake, and the holly wreath, and the toy duck?"

"I'm sorry," said Simon, "I couldn't help it somehow. It just happened."

"What happened?" asked Deborah sharply.

"Well," said Simon, "just after I went around the first turn in the road I found a child sitting on that big white rock, crying. He was about two or three years old, and I stopped and asked him why he was crying. He didn't answer. Then I told him not to cry like that, and I patted his head, but that didn't do any good, I hung around, trying to think up something, and I decided to put the cake down and take him up in my arms for a minute. But the cake slipped out of my hands and hit the rock, and a piece of the icing chipped off. Well, I thought, that baby in Bethlehem won't miss a little piece of icing, and I gave it to the child and he stopped crying. But when he finished he began to cry again. I just sort of squeezed another little piece of icing off and that was all right, for a little while; but then I had to give him another piece, and things went on that way, and all of a sudden I found that there wasn't any cake left. After that he looked as if he might cry again, and I didn't have any more cake and so I showed him the duck and he said 'Ta-ta.' I just meant to lend him the duck for a minute, but he wouldn't give it up. I coaxed him a good while, but he wouldn't let go. And then a woman came out of that little house and she began to scold him for staying out so late, and so I told her it was my fault and I gave her the holly wreath just so she wouldn't be mad at the child. And after that, you see, I didn't have anything to take to Bethlehem, and so I came back here."

Deborah had begun to cry long before Simon finished his story, but when he had done she lifted up her head and said, "How could you do it, Simon? Those presents were meant for the King of the World, and you gave them to the first crying child you met on the road."

Then she began to cry again, and Simon did not know what to say or do, and it grew darker and darker in the room and the fire on the hearth faded to a few embers. And that little red glow was all there was in the room. Now, Simon could not even see Deborah across the room, but he could still hear her sobbing. But suddenly the room was flooded with light and Deborah's sobbing broke into a great gulp and she rushed to the window and looked out. The stars danced in the sky and from high above the house came the voice of angels saying, "Glory to God in the highest, and on earth peace, good will toward men."

Deborah dropped to her knees in a panic of joy and fear. Simon knelt beside her, but first he said, "I thought maybe that the baby in Bethlehem wouldn't mind so very much."

A SONG

to be sung with an Eggnog in One Hand
and a String of Colored Lights in the Other

Whatever's happened to Christmas?
It occurs so often now!
When I was six or a little bit more,
Though we popped the corn and we wreathed the door,
Though we trimmed the tinseled bough,
That festival morn, that midnight clear—
They only enveloped us once a year.
While now as the world and I grow older,
Christmas keeps peering 'round my shoulder.

When I was seven or maybe eight,
The year crawled past like a snow-bound freight.
Centuries yawned, I well remember,
Between December and next December.

But now I'm grown-up, more or less,
The Yule pulls in like a fast express.
St. Nick's forever cutting a caper.
I'm always knee-deep in tissue paper.

Wherever I look, whenever I listen,
The joy-bells ring and the gift-cards glisten.
While last year's candles are still aglow,
I'm kissed under this year's mistletoe.

I've scarcely, at Macy's, exchanged in snatches,
The monogrammed coasters, the monogrammed matches,
When over again like seasonal symbols
The monogrammed scarves appear at Gimbel's.

The tree comes down. But I barely wheedle
Out of my carpet the trodden needle,
When janitors aping good will toward men
Are hinting for holiday tips again.

Noël has bound me in chains and fetters.
Just as I'm starting my thank-you letters,
Carols over the radio hummeth
And greetings fly and the mailman cometh.

Oh, twelve were the days of Christmas.
But that was a long time back.
For now so swiftly do they arrive,
It's more like three hundred sixty-five
In my personal almanac.
And somehow I find it melancholy—
To be always decking the halls with holly.
I might love Christmas a bushel and a peck
Would it only stop breathing down my neck.

PHYLLIS MCGINLEY

AN ODE of the BIRTH of OUR SAVIOR

In Numbers, and but these few,
I sing Thy Birth, Oh JESU!
Thou prettie Babie, borne here,
With sup'rabundant scorn here:
Who for Thy Princely Port here,
   Hadst for Thy place
    Of Birth, a base
Out-stable for thy Court here.

Instead of neat Inclosures
Of inter-woven Osiers;
Instead of fragrant Posies
Of Daffadills, and Roses;
Thy cradle, Kingly Stranger,
   As Gospel tells,
    Was nothing els,
But, here, a homely manger.

But we with Silks, (not Cruells)
With sundry precious Jewells,
And Lilly-work will dresse Thee;
And as we dispossesse thee
Of clouts, wee'l make a chamber,
   Sweet Babe, for Thee,
    Of Ivorie,
And plaister'd round with Amber.

The Jewes they did disdaine Thee,
But we will entertaine Thee
With Glories to await here
Upon Thy Princely State here,
And more for love, than pittie.
   From yeere to yeere
    Wee'l make Thee, here,
A free-born of our Citie.

ROBERT HERRICK

THE OXEN

Christmas Eve, and twelve of the clock.
 'Now they are all on their knees,'
An elder said as we sat in a flock
 By the embers in hearthside ease.

We pictured the meek mild creatures where
 They dwelt in their strawy pen,
Nor did it occur to one of us there
 To doubt they were kneeling then.

So fair a fancy few would weave
 In these years! Yet, I feel,
If someone said on Christmas Eve,
 'Come; see the oxen kneel,

'In the lonely barton by yonder coomb
 Our childhood used to know,'
I should go with him in the gloom,
 Hoping it might be so.

THOMAS HARDY

OUR JOYFUL FEAST

So, now is come our joyfulst feast,
*   Let every man be jolly;*
Each room with ivy leaves is drest,
*   And every post with holly.*
Though some churls at our mirth repine,
Round your foreheads garlands twine;
Drown sorrow in a cup of wine,
*   And let us all be merry.*

Now all our neighbour's chimnies smoke,
*   And Christmas logs are burning;*
Their ovens they with baked meats choke,
*   And all their spits are turning.*
Without the door let sorrow lie;
And if for cold it hap to die,
We'll bury't in a Christmas pie,
*   And evermore be merry.*

Now every lad is wondrous trim,
*   And no man minds his labour;*
Our lasses have provided them
*   A bog-pipe and a tabor;*
Young men and maids, and girls and boys,
Give life to one another's joys;
And you anon shall by their noise
*   Perceive that they are merry.*

Rank misers now do sparing shun;
*   Their hall of music soundeth;*
And dogs thence with whole shoulders run,
*   So all things there aboundeth.*
The country folks themselves advance
For crowdy-mutton's come out of France;
And Jack shall pipe, and Jill shall dance,
*   And all the town be merry.*
GEORGE WITHER

from TO THE CHILD JESUS

Could every time-worn heart but see Thee once again,
A happy human child, among the homes of men,
The age of doubt would pass,—the vision of Thy face
Would silently restore the childhood of the race.
HENRY VAN DYKE

OLD CHRISTMAS RETURNED

All you that to feasting and mirth are inclined,
Come here is good news for to pleasure your mind,
Old Christmas is come for to keep open house,
He scorns to be guilty of starving a mouse.
Then come, boys, and welcome for diet the chief,
Plum-pudding, goose, capon, minced pies, and
*   roast beef.*

The holly and ivy about the walls wind
And show that we ought to our neighbors be kind,
Inviting each other for pastime and sport,
And where we best fare, there we most do resort;
We fail not of victuals, and that of the chief,
Plum-pudding, goose, capon, minced pies, and
*   roast beef.*

All travellers, as they do pass on their way,
At gentlemen's halls are invited to stay,
Themselves to refresh, and their horses to rest,
Since that he must be Old Christmas's guest;
Nay, the poor shall not want, but have for relief,
Plum-pudding, goose, capon, minced pies, and
*   roast beef.*
TRADITIONAL

ROSEMARY

Beauty and Beauty's son and rosemary—
Venus and Love, her son, to speak plainly—
born of the sea supposedly,
at Christmas each, in company,
braids a garland of festivity.
  Not always rosemary—
since the flight to Egypt, blooming differently.
With lancelike leaf, green but silver underneath,
its flowers—white originally—
turned blue. The herb of memory,
imitating the blue robe of Mary,
  is not too legendary

to flower both as symbol and as pungency.
Springing from stones beside the sea,
the height of Christ when thirty-three—
not higher—it feeds on dew and to the bee
"hath a dumb language"; is in reality
  a kind of a Christmas-tree

                    MARIANNE MOORE

CHRISTMAS PRAYER

Lord, give our hearts their youth at Christmastide;
Let us believe, as did the three who went
To lay their gifts, their honor, and their pride
Before a Child. We who have richly spent
The coin of years need now replenished store
Of simple faith and hearts that seek the light.
We, too, would stand beside an open door,
To see the glow that circled earth's deep night.
Lord, help us find again the long-lost way
That led to wonder: in the welcome glow
From friendly windows, something of the gay
Comradely spirit we used to know.
The star shines on for those with eyes to see:
A finite gleam toward all infinity.
                    ELEANOR ALLETTA CHAFFE

CHRISTMAS SONG

Why do bells for Christmas ring?
Why do little children sing?

Once a lovely, shining star,
Seen by shepherds from afar,
Gently moved until its light
Made a manger-cradle bright.

There a darling Baby lay
Pillowed soft upon the hay.
And his mother sang and smiled,
"This is Christ, the Holy Child."

So the bells for Christmas ring,
So the little children sing.

                    LYDIA A. C. WARD

Christmastime is coming round.
Geese are getting fat,
Please to put a penny
In an old man's hat!
If you haven't got a penny
A ha'penny will do,
If you haven' got a ha'penny,
God
        bless
            you!

                    NURSERY RHYME

What Child Is This?

William C. Dix   Old English "Greensleeves"

Not too fast

1. What Child is this,_ Who, laid to rest,_ On Ma-ry's lap_ is
2. Why lies He in_ such mean es-tate,_ Where ox and ass_ are

sleep-ing? Whom an-gels greet with an-thems sweet, While shep-herds watch_ are keep-ing?
feed-ing? Good Chris-tians, fear: for sin-ners here_ The si-lent Word_ is plead-ing:

CHORUS

This,   this_ is Christ the King,_ Whom shep-herds guard_ and an-gels sing:
Nails,   spear,_ shall pierce Him through, The Cross be borne_ for me, for you:

Haste, haste_ to bring Him laud,_ The Babe,_ the Son_ of Ma-ry!
Hail,   hail,_ the Word made flesh,_ The Babe,_ the Son_ of Ma-ry!

O Come, All Ye Faithful

Latin Hymn

John Reading, 1692

With spirit, but not too fast

1. O come, all ye faithful, joyful and triumphant, O come ye, O come ye to Bethlehem: Come and behold Him, born the King of angels: O come, let us adore Him, O come, let us adore Him, O come, let us adore Him, Christ the Lord.

1. Adeste fideles, laeti triumphantes, Venite, Venite in Bethlehem: Natum videte, Regem angelorum: Venite adoremus, Venite adoremus, Venite adoremus, Dominum.

Traditional

God Rest You Merry, Gentlemen

Traditional English

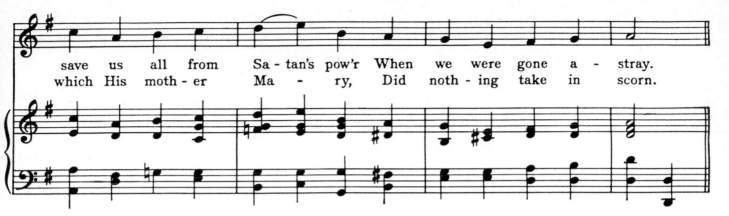

save us all from Sa - tan's pow'r When we were gone a - stray.
which His moth - er Ma - ry, Did noth - ing take in scorn.

CHORUS

O___ ti - dings of com - fort and joy, com - fort and

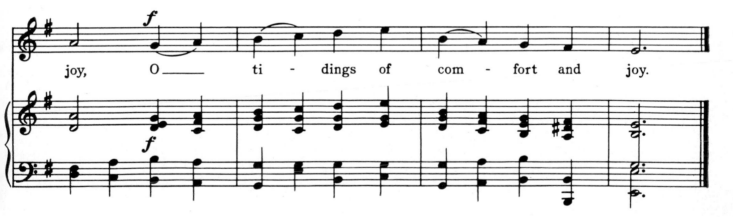

joy, O___ ti - dings of com - fort and joy.

From God our heav'nly Father,
  A blessed angel came,
And unto certain shepherds
  Brought tidings of the same;
How that in Bethlehem was born
  The Son of God by name.
    CHORUS

The shepherds at those tidings
  Rejoiced much in mind,
And left their flocks a-feeding,
  In tempest, storm, and wind:
And went to Bethlehem straightway,
  The Son of God to find.
    CHORUS

John M. Neale

Good King Wenceslas

Piae Cantiones, 1582

1. Good king Wen - ces - las look'd out, On the Feast of
2. "Hith - er, page, and stand by me, If thou know'st it,

Steph - en, When the snow lay round a - bout,
tell - ing, Yon - der peas - ant, who is he?

Deep and crisp and e - ven: Bright - ly shone the
Where and what his dwell - ing?" "Sire, he lives a

moon that night, Though the frost was cru - el, When a poor man
good league hence, Un - der - neath the moun - tain; Right a - gainst the

came in sight, Gath - 'ring win - ter fu - el.
for - est fence, By Saint Ag - nes' foun - tain".

"Bring me flesh, and bring me wine,
  Bring me pine logs hither,
Thou and I will see him dine,
  When we bear them thither."
Page and monarch forth they went,
  Forth they went together;
Through the rude winds' wild lament,
  And the bitter weather.

"Sire, the night is darker now,
  And the wind blows stronger;
Fails my heart, I know not how,
  I can go no longer."
"Mark my footsteps, my good page,
  Tread thou in them boldly:
Thou shalt find the winter's rage
  Freeze thy blood less coldly."

In his master's steps he trod,
  Where the snow lay dinted;
Heat was in the very sod
  Which the saint had printed.
Therefore, Christian men, be sure,
  Wealth or rank possessing,
Ye who now will bless the poor,
  Shall yourselves find blessing.

Hark! The Herald Angels Sing

Charles Wesley, 1739

Mendelssohn, 1840

1. Hark! the her-ald an-gels sing,_ Glo-ry to the new-born King; Peace on earth and
2. Christ, by high-est heav'n a-dored, Christ, the ev-er-last-ing Lord; Late in time be-

mer-cy mild,_ God and sin-ners re-con-ciled! Joy-ful all ye na-tions, rise,_
hold Him come,_ Off-spring of the Vir-gin's womb. Veil'd in flesh the God-head see,_

Join the tri-umph of the skies;_ With th'an-gel-ic host pro-claim Christ is_born in
Hail th'In-car-nate De-i-ty,___ Pleased as Man with man to dwell, Je-sus_ our Em-

REFRAIN

Beth-le-hem. Hark! the her-ald an-gels sing, Glo-ry_ to the new-born King.
man-u-el!

Away in a Manger

Martin Luther   German

To the Christian world, the Bible is the word of God and therefore Christ is His Son as described in stories of the birth as told by the apostles. The spirit of this annual celebration is captured beautifully in the symbolism of the Bible opened on an altar pedestal and glorified with the glow of a foil collage and lighted tapers.

The medieval practice of representing the Lord as the "Light of the World" by a burning candle is preserved in the liturgy of Christian churches today. The rose, an emblem of love and beauty, is dedicated to the Virgin Mary.

CHRISTMAS SYMBOLS

Since the fifth century, Christians have been celebrating the birth of Christ. Time has changed some of the methods and has added new customs, but the original intention remains the same—the symbolic representation of the Holy Birth. Each of the elements surrounding that simple birth over two thousand years ago, the manger, the magi, the ox and ass, and many more, plays an important part in our Christmas today as a symbol of that night and of future events in the life of Christ and that for which he stood.

Custom is often perpetuated long after its true meaning and origin have been forgotten. Few celebrations retain as many symbols with their true significance as Christmas. Recalling the meanings of the symbols gives Christmas its special flavor and has helped to maintain the purport of this Holy Christian celebration of the birth of Christ.

Manger scenes are common sights in homes decorated for the holidays. The scene portrays the actual event as interpreted by an artist or craftsman. The earliest known Nativity scene served as a burial chamber decoration in the catacombs of Rome. The crude manger and setting represent humility and the grave swaddling clothes refer to His future suffering. St. Francis of Assisi was the first to use the manger with figure sculpture as a Christmas shrine.

The shepherds were the first known worshipers of Christ. The sheep, worshiping Christ with the shepherds, are lowly creatures often used to symbolize humanity with Christ as the divine Shepherd.

Exchanging gifts is a custom dating to the ancient Romans. After the birth of Christ and the incident of the gift-bearing Magi, the practice was adapted to the Christmas celebration. The gift-giving custom symbolizes love.

The "gift-giver" has many faces and is individualized with each country. In many countries the child Jesus is the gift-giver while in others an unusual figure impersonates the gift-bringer. In Italy, La Befana, distributes the presents, in Russia, Babushka delivers them, and in the United States it is Santa.

Three Kings came, too, to worship the new-born King. The Wise Men, or Magi, visited the manger after the birth. Their visit was foretold in Psalm 71 and Isaiah 60 as kings bearing gifts of frankincense and gold for the Savior.

Bethlehem is the city in which Christ was born. Caesar Augustus decreed that a census be taken and each man go to his own town to register. Joseph, of the house of David, traveled to Bethlehem where Mary give birth to Christ.

Angels appeared to the shepherds near Bethlehem telling of the birth of Christ and praising God. Angels are often given musical instruments in pictorial representations in the assumption that they sang the praises of God that first Christmas eve.

The star above the manger was the symbol of divine guidance. God led those who would believe to the birthplace of His Son. The ox and ass illustrate the humblest and least of creation recognizing and worshiping Christ as the Son of God.

Mary and the Infant Jesus have symbolized the Incarnation since early in Christian art. The apple, present in many pictorial and sculptural works, symbolizes the fall of man, and the redemption coming from Christ.

The halo surrounding the heads of Mary and Jesus indicate glory or holiness and the radiant light which God had sent to the earth.

DOORWAYS

A front door introduction to the holiday gaiety within—what better way to let friends and neighbors know that you have the Christmas spirit? And dressing your door is a perfect way to begin the holidays. Let Christmas begin there and spread throughout the rest of your house. The Christmas spirit is infectious and the designs shown on the next pages can help touch off neighborhood participation. Select one, adapt it, and watch the spirit spread!

A "well-dressed" door does not need to cost a lot of money. Use whatever is handy and seasonal around the house. Use fabric remnants, Christmas ribbon; cover shapely hatboxes; cut tin can lids into shiny flowers, or twist the rims into tree forms; make paper trees from last year's gift paper. Tasteful designing need not entail buying numerous new items.

Remember that the decoration you choose to grace your door will welcome all those who come in sight. It is prophetic of the amity they will find inside. If your hospitality is warm and casual, you might fix your door to indicate this with a perky Santa or impish cherubs. If your rooms have an old-world charm and symmetry, try a traditional wreath or simple garland. Christmas is a time of fun and laughter, of anticipation and planning, and the most fun comes before December 26.

These doorway welcomers use honest-to-goodness fruit. Dozens of polished and shiny apples on florist picks, stick into wire-covered plastic foam cone bases. Variegated holly and sprigs of fir fill and cover the crevices and keep fresh and green in the slightly dampened plastic foam. Florist clay and masking tape anchor the trees to the urn-like cast concrete jardinieres.

Lush evergreen wreath shown below surrounds a center wreath of straw. The straw wreath has a frame backing covered by gold burlap which is finished around the rim by gold braid. Wide red plastic bow passes behind the center wreath.

A straw angel adorns the center wreath. It's made of straws in conical form with upper ends trimmed as wings.

Strips of green burlap overlaid with evergreen boughs (above) frame this wide doorway. Punctuating greenery are red satin streamers, caught in three places with bunches of artificial apples, red peppers. Jeweled lutes add finish at top.

A simple ribbon treatment on a slab door looks effective when the design is repeated on the inside. If you have a glass area near your entrance, as shown below, place the tree there. The lights give an inviting glow to the glass.

An effective, yet relatively easy door embellishment to achieve is the one at right. To reproduce this design at your entry, attach pairs of wide red velvet ribbon strips to the top and bottom of the door, or, if you like, continue the strips on the inside of the door for a duplicate treatment on the inside. Add artificial magnolia leaves or real ones you sprayed yourself.

If there's a light fixture nearby, trim it with velvet ribbon and greens to repeat the color theme of the door.

Traditional Christmas colors combine with a modern look to make the door decoration below. Make by using a hatbox cut in half, covering the rounded portions with red velvet edged by green and gold braid. Green velvet ribbon in 1-inch widths forms handles for the containers. Cardboard closes open backs with invisible mending tape. Wide red velvet bows top handles.

Greens, pine cones, large tree baubles fill the insides of the containers. Small packages or Christmas cards could be added instead.

To make above plaques, cut three circles of cardboard with 10-, 12-, and 14-inch diameters. Spray-paint circles or cover with fabric. Cut and cover four triangles for each circle. You'll need four with 2½″ sides, four with 6″ sides, and four with 7″ sides. Tape triangles together to form diamonds, cover outer edges with braid, fasten to circles. Top plaques with bows.

Three hatbox lids, at right, attached to 4-foot wood dowel or garden stick, combine to create this seasonal topiary door design.

Lids and shaft have red and green cotton velvet covers, but felt would be just as effective. In the center of each lid, wire half a plastic-foam ball. Decorate with glittered dowel sticks and with small glass Christmas baubles.

Cherubic angels decorate this double doorway in a simple, yet appealing manner. Angels are easy to reproduce and may easily be varied in trim and size.

To copy angels, enlarge pattern below to desired size. Trace onto medium-weight cardboard or plywood. Cut around tracing, then decorate angel shapes with paper, metal foil, fabric, or paint. Add wire to back for hanging.

1 SQ=2 INCHES

Happy-go-lucky toy soldier with hands on his hips, needs plenty of room to stand guard in front of your house. He's six feet tall.

Use him by your fireplace during wet weather, other times, let him flank your entry to protect a giant basket of gifts wrapped especially for guests invited to a party.

To copy tall soldier that was only one of a long row of soldiers in a store-window display, you need very few materials—pine 2x4s, poster paint, gold foil, a feather and a few feet of lightweight corrugated cardboard (the kind used in packing various kinds of breakable items).

After the design materials are collected, build a wood framework and wrap the corrugated body—the soldier could be smaller.

Once corrugated cardboard is positioned, staple it along the seam to hold. Spray-paint the soldier using masking tape to delineate areas. Add separate belt and arms. Accessorize with metal foil buckle and braid, feather for cap.

Hootenanny door, below, was designed to reflect the musical interests of the family. Evergreen branches are attached to the square panels of the door, then topped with a variety of toy musical instruments at the dime store, and gilded for a uniform appearance. Toy drums are actually one-pound coffee tins covered with red wool. Other decorative details include the large red velvet bow gracing the center panels. Sleigh bells stream down from the bow.

You could adapt this idea to display one of your own family's particular interests, if the musical theme doesn't reflect your personality.

A beautiful Christmas card was the inspiration for this artful presentation above of the Three Kings bearing gifts.

Three kings were positioned to face and to complement the Spanish Colonial door with its hand-carved regional design.

Make these kings by enlarging the designs from a favorite card onto white dress box cardboard. After cutting out the figures, sketch in the robes and crowns. Make two holes in each cardboard figure, then run pieces of garden wire through to the back to attach to a wire-covered wooden frame.

Each garment is made from different kinds of fabric oddments of felt, velvet, silk, and taffeta. Trimmings include embroidered tapes, ribbons. Pearls, sequins, and jewels decorate crowns. Two cotton beards are white, the other one is sprayed gold.

Make a frame of 1x2s to fit space or area you'll cover and attach poultry wire across the opening. Long-needled pine boughs fastened to the wire with pieces of garden wire make the mat for the background.

Tin rosettes and pine cones, below, are combined in this gold-sprayed wreath. Rosettes are made of ends cut from various sizes of tin cans. You'll need tin snips, scratch awl, and long-nosed pliers. Cut six slashes to ½ inch of the center of each lid. Arrange four or five with the smallest on top.

With awl, punch two holes ¼ inch apart at center. Wire lids together, then wire unit to a firm support. Using pliers (and gloves), curl and crimp petals until you have a "rose."

Coffee-can rings are the main materials for the distinctive design above. Rings are individually wrapped with green ribbon, then joined with the same ribbon. Gold leaves and ornaments are tied on.

Slate gray door trimmed in white accents the big plaid bow centering this natural green wreath, at left. Bright red glass ornaments add color and shine to the decoration. A hurricane lamp at the front steps can be added to highlight the ornaments.

Evergreen wreath, above, that you make or buy can be brightened with this treatment. Use olive green satin ribbon for trim. Make angels of red paper, adding paper faces, hair, wings, and trim for robes.

Six miniature trees march in precision up one side and across the top of a bright red door, above. Each tree consists of five wood flowerpot labels glued into shape, painted blue and white. Top with foil stars.

Topiary of boxwood on red background is easy to make. Sprigs of boxwood and holly berries are inserted into pieces of plastic foam. Tree stem is lengths of 1-inch dowel painted white. Semicircular flowerpot is white papier-mache. Wire or glue components to red covered panel.

Novel door decoration shown above is sure to be an attention-getter. Begin with a gold-sprayed straw garden hat, wire sprigs of evergreen under brim, add plastic leaves, paper flowers, and a bow.

Artificial apples and pine sprigs wired to a flat rattan tree are elements of this door adornment, above. Fasten the tree to your door and frame it with long streamers from a giant green bow fastened above.

Gold topiary, right, on green panel has cover of boxwood, sprays of ivy. Boxwood, ivy, and artificial roses are wired to florist picks which are inserted in 10-inch semi-sphere of plastic foam, and in papier-mache pot. Spray gold before adding roses, ivy, birds. Stem is length of 1-inch dowel.

Children's garden tools create this gardener's back door design. Bells are small flowerpots. Spray tools, pots with flat white paint, powder with mica snow while paint is still wet. Red oilcloth makes bow.

Strawflowers, seedpods, and artificial holly berries are used for this handsome door swag. Begin with half of a plastic foam cone fastened to cardboard backing. Arrange strings of berries, rows of flowers, rows of seed pods barber-pole fashion up the cone, and add a stained plywood base. Glue or pin unit to 4½-inch looped satin ribbons attached to small brass ring.

Large kickshaws, left, covered with burlap make dramatic door accents during the holidays. The basic yuletide shapes were cut from heavy cardboard. Then various hues of burlap were cut the same shape with a 1-inch border to allow for folding over the edge. Shapes were also notched at points and curves to allow for a smooth fit. Excess fabric was trimmed off.

The burlap was glued to the fronts of the shapes, with the allowance folded over and glued to the back. Masking tape covers ragged edges.

Fabric loops attached to drapery rings were glued to tops for hanging, then brown paper was glued over the backs of the shapes. Gold and silver paper doilies were cut and glued on the faces of the ornaments to create design interest, as were other knickknacks such as discarded jewelry, sequins, felt, and rickrack. Dimensions of these designs include 19-inch star, 29-inch teardrop, 23½-inch tree, 23-inch diamond.

FIREPLACES

From the warmth of a fireplace, decked with evergreens, lavish red bows, stockings, and candles, come extra felicitations at Christmas. From stockings hung on the mantel to garlands hung on the wall above, the tradition of fireplace decorating has special meaning to many families. The fireplace is often the focal point of a room and the trims on it can set the theme for the whole house.

Naturally, the decorations should fit the size and style of the fireplace. A simple colonial fireplace like the one on the left needs traditional materials—evergreens, candles, antiques. A more modern, severe fireplace demands simple, austere ornamentation. The fireplace adornments should be chosen with care. Let them reflect the personality of the house and family—then the fireplace will radiate holiday warmth.

A candlelighted, espaliered tree next to a crackling fire sets the mood for this inviting Christmas morning scene. Each tree branch holds clusters of white blossoms and greens that conceal plastic foam holders for red candles. Baubles snuggle into evergreens above fireplace.

Antiques surround this rustic fireplace. Evergreens and holly leaves and berries top wooden mantel lined with pewter candle holders and bright red candles. The greens, holly, and berries are repeated in the iron and copper pieces placed directly above fire and on the deck.

54

Simple but effective settings such as at right are designed for the whole family to enjoy. Evergreen sprigs with small figurines and old candlesticks grace the mantel beam. In the fireplace "oven" above the woodbox, a miniature nativity scene is at a low eye-level for children to enjoy. The traditional wreath of evergreen with red bow and small baubles occupies the place of honor above the fireplace.

The Della Robbia wreath above this mantel, left, is mounted on a 24-inch plywood disk ½-inch thick. Wires pass through three pairs of holes behind the doll representing the Christ-child. Wind wires over doll's body, twist tight in back.

Evergreen swags across the fireplace breast are fastened to heavy wire or straightened coat hangers to give the shape. On heavy wire, fasten greens and fruit with transparent tape or light wire around stems.

Handsome pewter collection of graduate-size measuring mugs and large charger plates becomes the center of interest for this setting.

Branches of evergreen and metallic red roping are arranged around the pewter pieces to create a close-knit effect. Milking can on hearth, rare candle box, the rocker, settle, and hooked rug all combine to make warm charm of country room.

You can substitute a collection of other rare pieces, such as china or brass items, for the pewter collection shown here. Also effective on a high mantel such as this, would be a grouping of antique wooden toys, or replicas of tree ornaments used during the Colonial period.

Old and new, left, combine to create a simple hearth scene. The imaginative designer salvaged old newel posts from porch railing, transformed them into handsome candlesticks. Massive beeswax candles top each of the posts. Pine boughs with extra long needles are in proper proportion to the giant candlesticks and add needed color.

Antique German bust, sitting on a wall-hung "pedestal" tops the triangular-shaped holiday design.

Old split fieldstone fireplace, left, topped by an aged lintel beam becomes the center of interest in this inviting Christmas scene. The room illustrates how cherished heirloom pieces may be used during the holiday season.

Here we see simple swags used above the hearth, with the tree given a place of importance near the fireplace, and in conversation grouping.

Gentle tones of complementary colors, right, create a rich setting for this mantel grouping of green and gold. Molding on pickled pine wall paneling frames a wreath bearing gold-sprayed fruit and a pair of "branching" ornamented candlesticks.

An old-fashioned rocking horse, below, sans rockers and its own nursery home, plus old newel posts salvaged from an urban redevelopment flotsam, combine with baskets, greens, ribbons, and showy white paint to become a sight to delight visitors of all ages. While this pony is solid wood, a modern version in plastic or metal could be substituted.

To copy horse, sand any blemished areas, then spray paint everything snowy white. Brush mane, tail, and stockings with gold paint; brush eyes, saddle trim, and hoofs with black paint. Now paint reins and saddle red, apply red flocking while paint is still wet. Areas

not to be flocked should be covered with masking tape and paper. When paint and flocking are dry, attach red yarn tassels to the handles.

Newel posts are sanded, spray painted white. The red felt strips are glued in place. Baskets sprayed white, edged in gold, sit atop the posts. Fill with plastic foam balls flocked in red and fresh holly leaves and pine cones flocked in brown then gilded to continue color theme

Holiday bell pull uses 3-inch velvet florist ribbon with gold braid glued down center. Miniature wreaths are tiny Austrian pine cones glued to cardboard rings, sprayed gold. Leaves are glycerined, clustered with artificial apples.

Warm yuletide atmosphere radiates from this authentic English inn room, above. The blazing fire accents beam mantel bedecked in Christmas greens and holly. Bright red candles, brass candlesticks, pewter heirlooms nestle in greens complementing antiqued reproduction of crest. Tall pine tree is dressed in traditional ropes of popcorn and cranberries. Accessories of bright red add the finishing touches to the room.

Heavy wire in a casual S shape creates the framework for this attractive decoration. Stars, leaves, and clusters of balls, all sprayed gold, are attached with fine wire. Design simplicity creates an effect complementary to the scale of the stonework and room.

The handsome frame for this simple treatment, above, is made of bottoms of egg cartons. Glue carton bottoms together and to narrow cardboard frame. Paint cartons gold and press green foil into depressions. Three figures, star, and greens complete design.

Corner fireplace at right is decorated with mammoth gold wreath, evergreen branches. The wreath (it's still beautiful after seven years' use) is constructed of pine cones, pods, and leaves collected from family vacations and trips. New discoveries are added each year, making the wreath grow in size and sentiment. Feathers and various glass trinkets mingle with the greenery.

For a large area above a fireplace, try the idea below. A rose trellis is put to winter use as a wall tree when inverted and tied with spruce branches. Red ornaments on wire stems are stapled on. The base is plastic foam wrapped with red paper.

Suspended Yule Log, above, gives a traditional air to this contemporary fireplace. The log is shaped from a piece of cedar bark, gently curled into position and wired to a perforated hardboard rectangle for support. Streamers of green satin-backed red ribbon wrap around log, English holly; pine cones wire in place for accent.

Contemporary fireplaces need trimming restraint as shown below. The uncluttered effect created by a giant arm of greens is complemented by the sparse adornments of pine cones and a bow completely in keeping with the sleek straight lines already established.

BIG TREES

Christmas is not Christmas without a tree to decorate with tinsel, popcorn chains, sparkling glass balls, and glittery stars, a tree under which to hide special presents for loved ones. And, although historians differ as to the origin of decorating the live, green tree, there can be no question about its importance during the yuletide, it has become such a widespread custom in our country.

Trees now come in all shapes, sizes, and colors. Some we cover with one-of-a-kind family heirlooms, some with all matching, one-color glass balls, and some with only white flocking. But no matter how they are decorated or with what, the sentiment that goes with decorating and with admiring the tree stays constant year after year after year.

Whether the decorating interpretation is modern, traditional, or futuristic, a tree can be trimmed with style. Choose the size carefully; consider the proportions of your room. Planning the colors and the kind of baubles to adorn the tree (do you already have a collection or do you need to replenish your supply) can make the difference between a "just right tree" and an ordinary one. Make it your tree exclusively and enjoy it.

Della Robbia styled wreaths enhance this immense tree. Wreaths have eight-inch diameter plastic foam rings smothered by artificial fruit glued to secure. Red bows add decorator touch.

Hollow plastic fruit from the dime store hangs from yarn for this Mexican theme tree. Cookie-thin plastic foam forms gingerbread men; crossed sticks wrapped in yarn form "God's eyes."

A traditional Christmas tree gets a new look by hanging customary ornaments in diamond- and star-shape frames that are made from lightweight cardboard. Either use cardboard which is all one color, or painted in several shades that harmonize with the balls used.

For the star shapes, cut a star-shape pattern from cardboard circles. Cut out centers slightly larger than the ornament to be framed. Hang an ornament in the center with fine wire or thread. Cut out diamond shapes from cardboard and cut out centers leaving 1/2 inch rims. Hang ornament in center. The double diamond shapes are scored and stapled in the center. Fold the diamonds lightly along the line away from each other making four wings 90° apart with the ball centered.

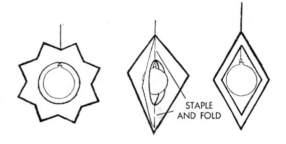

STAPLE AND FOLD

To create the geometric forms of cardboard on the handsome tree at left, mount four triangles four inches high and three inches across the base to a three-inch square, taping joints on the inside. Make a second pyramid; mask bases together on outside. Glue various shades of fabric to cardboard, edge with gold braid. Gild alternating sections with paint or gold glitter.

Pierce florists' wire through peak, loop over bough. Make graduated-size ornaments to hang on different levels on the Christmas tree.

Lively strips of felt add a bit of punch to Christmas decorating. The tree, trimmed with cheerful Yuletide greetings highlighted by small twinkle-lights, is set against a soft background of blue, brown, and gold. From the top of the wall, the strips, cut into various widths, hang down gently to the brick fireplace ledge where they are securely held by double-faced tape. The felt is then drawn out onto the floor to provide a perfect place for gaily wrapped presents.

For snug look, the tree required special tailoring. Before it was set into the corner the back was carefully pruned to fit flush against the wall. Because of its proximity to the fireplace, the tree was treated with fire retardant.

Dismantled commercial Christmas ornaments provide the material for baubles on this green tree.

Giant sunbursts have cardboard bases centered with small mirrors. Strings of small beads glued in layers encircle the mirrors forming the massive frames. Lightweight cardboard sunbeam points attach to the cardboard backing and snowflakes detached from the commercial flakes embellish the points. Silvery dust is sprayed over the design.

Flocked pipe cleaners wrapped around tree balls and twisted into curls form the cage-like ornaments. Beads threaded on pipe cleaners and a long pendant form the dangles. Red and white pipe cleaner angels dance from the branches.

Correlating the blues of the room, this magnificent tree fits serenely into the color scheme of the living area. Large and small balls covered with olive green and aqua satin hang from the white flocked tree branches. Tassels in matching blue, large foil poinsettias, and strings of blue foil complete the trim. The packages wrapped in blues and greens under the tree continue the color scheme.

Snowy white flocked tree with full branches presents a brightly colored sight for family and friends during the holidays.

Balanced atop branches are gay hued butterflies of red and orange, yellow and green. Butterflies are shaped of medium-weight cardboard used for posters. Teardrop shapes of colored paper are attached with white glue for designs.

Yards of swirling green net envelope this frosty white tree. The veiling net is cut into wide strips, then gathered slightly together as the fabric wraps around the tree.

Dark green ornament balls are given white ribs with paint. Green and white bows attach to the tops to match greens of the tree and net.

A red flocked tree for the holidays adds a bold accent to neutral walls and draperies in this room. Christmas-red ornaments of glass and store-bought white doves of papier mache are the tree's only ornaments, making a striking combination. Red and white gifts repeat colors.

In an old-fashioned tradition, this green tree is loaded with memorabilia collected throughout the years. The ornaments complement the color scheme of the family room and add special significance.

Large green velvet bows and bright blue and green balls repeat colors of emerald chair. Bright paper ornaments of toy soldiers, doves, and angels add color accent. Off-white drapery provides contrast.

TREE ORNAMENTS

A tree to decorate for Christmas—for your youngsters, for grandparents, for close friends, for a social or church group, or for yourself—can you imagine Christmas without it? And what fun it is to have a part in the decorating! Tree trinkets and baubles mean much more when each is handcrafted with care by someone you know or by you yourself.

Crafting materials can come from anywhere, from small boxes to round zipper containers. Cover them with felt or glue and glitter. And remember the size of your tree when making ornaments. Proportion is important to make everything just right. Plan, too, with the color scheme in mind of the room in which the tree will stand, and with the style of your decor, whether it is traditional, contemporary, or modern. A truly handsome tree is decorated with all that in mind and with all the care that goes with the season and reflects the special spirit.

Rainbow-colored felt partridges can be displayed as wall designs like the one shown below, or on a Christmas tree as ornaments. Cut two shapes for each bird using a pre-established pattern. Glue strips of metallic baby rickrack between the shapes to form the tail and head pieces. Finish the decoration by gluing on wings, sequin eyes, and other trim.

Make pears from a pattern and add round sequins and green leaves. Attach baby rickrack string to the tops to hang on the tree.

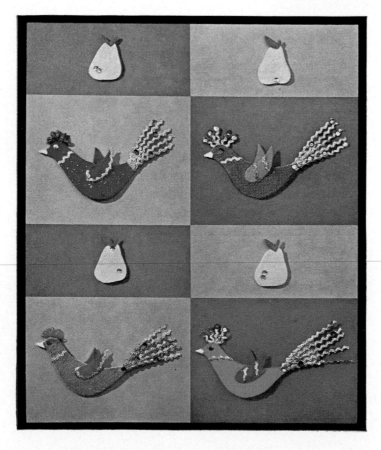

Ring out the joyous message of the season with these delightful starched sewing thread and rickrack bells, stars, and circles.

To begin the bells, brush a thin layer of rubber cement around edge of paper cup. (Use two cups if one is not firm enough.) Wrap mercerized thread around cup, first vertically then horizontally and again vertically. Wind baby rickrack over thread, being certain a strip is placed around bottom edge of bell. Dip bell in a heavy-finish starch solution (3-4 tablespoons of starch to 1 cup water). Let stand until dry (about 1-2 days).

Carefully cut out circle at bottom of bell; remove the paper cup. Lace a strip of middy braid through top of bell and make a knot inside. Use braid as hanger.

Glue sequins on sides of circle cut from cup bottom. Hang with an ornament hook.

To make mercerized star, cut a cardboard circle. Wrap thread approximately 18 times around each arm of star. Tuck in loose thread ends. Dip stars in starch and let dry. Insert a pencil under the threads on one side; turn over star; insert scissors under the threads; cut to center of cardboard. Repeat for other side. Pull out cardboard gently, hang with thread to tree ornament hook.

Household foil wrap combines with gelatin molds to make tree ornaments. To copy, line the inside of molds with foil by pressing in place with fingers or eraser end of a pencil, leaving extra edging. Crush more foil, fill in rest of the mold. Glue cut-to-shape felt to overlap the foil. Duplicate the process for the other side of the ornament. Glue the sides together and trim.

Key chains double as ornaments when decorated with felt and sewing trim. First chain is made by wrapping 18-inch strips of middy braid, folded in half, around a pearl. Glue four together. Third chain is made similarly with jewels covering the center hole. Second and fourth are plastic holders covered with felt; decorated with ribbon, rickrack, and middy braid. Last is made from folded middy braid.

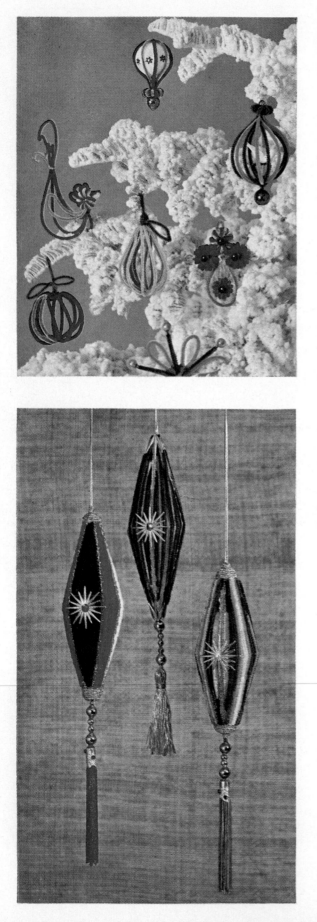

To create chenille trifles for tree flocked white or green, mold 12-inch chenille stems to desired shape. Draw stems together where necessary; secure them with wire or another stem. Curl stem ends by twisting them around a pencil. Add beads, plastic foam balls, sequins, or glass baubles for finishing details.

Perky and gay tree decorations below are made by gluing yarn in four colors around a cardboard cylinder. Each stripe measures about 1 inch wide. Cotton fringe balls edge bottom. Yarn loop serves as hanger.

Easy-to-make baubles on the right hold tiny gifts, as well as grace the tree. To create them, machine-stitch or glue felt, velvet, or velveteen covers to fit over small boxes, cups, or cans. Leave a space open for inserting and removing gifts. Trim trinkets with bangles, buttons, ribbons, sequins, tinsel, and beads.

Diamond-shaped ornaments have plastic foam cones held together by florist picks. Ends of florist chenille insert into apexes of baubles. Gold braid is glued along lengths of cones, around apexes. Foil stars attach to ornaments which suspend from chenille hangers tipped in glue and inserted into the ornament tops. Tassels connected to strings of beads attach to bottoms.

Flaming pinks and oranges of crisp tissue paper flowers look all the more exciting for their frosty background. This view shows how each was put together.

1 Cut colored tissue paper into pieces measuring 5x10 inches. Fold in half to get 5 inches square; refold twice more for 2½-inch squares. Refold in triangle.

Next, cut guide in the shape of half a heart, as shown in sketch below. Trace half-heart shape onto folded triangle and cut out.

2 Lay one set of petals on top of the other so they overlap. Touch with glue at center to secure shreds of colored tissue resembling flower stamens. Insert pin through center and attach bloom to plastic foam ball. Cover ball completely with flowers. Attach streamers.

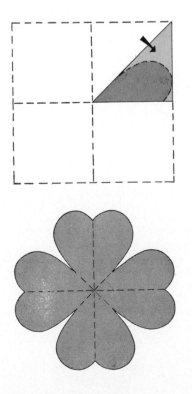

Make-believe flowers hand crafted from colorful tissues and pipe cleaners give individuality and innovation to this tree. Bend pipe cleaners in petal shapes. Fasten ends securely by slipknotting strong thread. Glue one side of pipe cleaner leaf to tissue paper, cutting around edge when dry. Push petal into plastic foam ball. Add chenille cleaners on center and around edge for variation.

Candy canes in three sizes fasten at top with masking tape covered with document seal to make angel. Plastic foam head has bead crown, foil star eyes, pipe cleaner neck. Wings are foil.

Miniature reproductions of figures from children's literature will brighten any tree on which they hang. And the nice thing about them is that they may be made at home, using balsa wood, matchsticks, toothpicks, sucker sticks, wire, cardboard, cork, plastic, wood filler, rope, or most anything that is handy. To hang them on the tree, punch a tiny hole through the soft wood and string monofilament through.

Little Red Riding Hood ornament strolls through this tiny village nestled in a wooded area. The tree baubles are carved from balsa wood. Their trunks are shaped from twigs and sucker sticks, then glued into small holes drilled on undersides. Tree heights range from $2\frac{1}{2}$ to 3 inches. They are decorated with bright green enamel paints.

Village house ornaments are carved of solid pieces of balsa. The roof of the gingerbread house is thin balsa wood that has been frosted by running wood filler across top to form ripples, then painted with white enamel paint. Bits of paper and toothpicks decorate the sides which are then painted. The outside houses have roofs cut from plastic foam cups.

Little Red Riding Hood stands about $2\frac{1}{2}$ inches tall. She is formed of scraps of wood glued together and decorated. Her clothes and body are painted with bright colored enamels.

The Nativity story, illustrated by miniature wooden ornaments made by hand, will add special meaning to the tree on which they hang. Or they could sit in a prominent spot on a mantel or end table. The Three Shepherds and Three Wise Men at the left can be the first pieces in the collection. Add the rest later, or add one new piece a year.

All six figures begin with 2¾-inch-tall nun dolls purchased at the dime store. To the shepherds are added arms carved from a wood dowel with a small diameter (⅛ to ½ inch). The sheep are carved entirely from balsa. Fine wire crooks are attached through arms to complete the attire.

To the kings are added tiny gifts carved from balsa wood and crowns made from shaped paper and more carved wood. After all of the accessories are glued in place, each figure is deftly painted with colorful enamel paints. For tiny markings, use a fine watercolor brush.

To hang them on a tree, thread monofilament or thread through a tiny hole punctured in the top. Secure the thread and wood with a dab of wood filler. Paint over the filler to disguise it.

"Little Jack Horner" sits inside a catalog-ordered cardboard sphere frosted with tissue, tiny chunks of plastic foam and mica flakes. Carved balsa body is topped with a wood bead head. Wood dowel arms and legs attach with glue. Tree, base, bench, and wreath are all carved balsa. Sand until smooth and paint. Glue in position on tiny stage.

"Old Mother Hubbard" goes to a carved balsa cupboard with painted china plates, cups, and saucers. Cupboard glues onto the stage corner. Mother Hubbard is a painted birthday candle holder and her doggy is carved balsa. Paint sphere walls with watercolor or cover them with a miniature fabric. Paint the stage floor in wood tones.

"Peter, Peter, Pumpkin Eater" stands on a small platform of thin balsa. After sealing the two-part ball, cut an opening and build the platform. Carved balsa forms Peter's pumpkin and insulating wire transforms into a curling vine. Peter is a candle holder with a wooden bead head and Peter's wife is a painted bead glued to the pumpkin.

"Mistress Mary, quite contrary" waters her garden with a tiny balsa sprinkling can. Paint the sky and grass, spot with clouds. Shape a flat balsa tree and cover with corduroy. Flat toothpicks glued together make the picket fence and paper and wood form the flowers. Use a bead and candle holder for Mary and paint the whole thing colorfully.

Lanterns of holiday red and green will add a lively touch of color and note of greeting throughout the house. And they don't require days to copy.

Make them in many sizes and papers; trim with wood beads, tree baubles, and plastic foam balls. Tint them with enameled paints and suspend them with string, wire, or thread from ceilings, trees, or doorways.

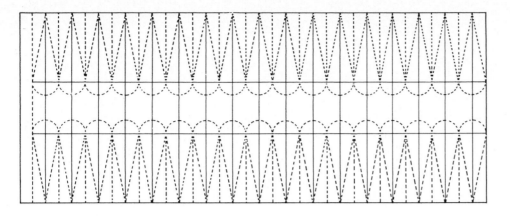

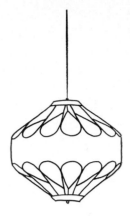

You'll enjoy making this handsome lantern; it's the easiest of the three shown. To copy lantern, start with a rectangle of paper 22x9½ inches. Reproduce lines indicated above, score along the broken lines, and fold in the direction indicated. Pull the pleats together, lace with thread. Connect side edges with glue or staples. Add bands of paper at the top and bottom to conceal thread. Attach hanging cord.

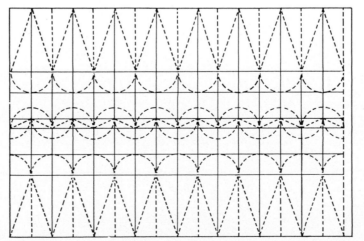

You can readily master the folds for this lantern, it's an elongated version of one above.

Begin with 27x16-inch rectangle of paper. Reproduce lines shown in drawing, score along broken lines, then fold neatly. Pull pleats together; secure with thread. Connect side edges as for the lantern above with glue or staples. Finish top and bottom with wood beads or glass baubles.

If you have completed the first two lanterns, you can easily breeze through this one, too.

Reproduce the pattern shown at right on a piece of paper still wider than the ones used for the first two designs . . . about 27x18 inches. You'll want to practice making the center scallops on scrap paper before making the finished lantern.

Complete the design with round wood beads, narrow paper, and a thread hanger.

For a test of imagination and creative skill, try designing variations of handsome hanging ornaments below made of lightweight cardboard. Attached to glass Christmas balls, they make a pleasing contrast to the commercial ornaments. Before attempting original designs, practice by making these.

For the center design, fold 9x12-inch piece of lightweight cardboard in half, or use a paper pattern first and trace on the cardboard. Copy the design and cut on continuous lines shown and fold on the broken lines. Roll design tips around a pencil to curl.

Left and right designs require two folds (the cardboard or paper should be folded into quarters). Place center of pattern on corner where all folds meet. Decorate the cutouts with glass beads, sequins, and rhinestones. Attach designs with glue to the balls.

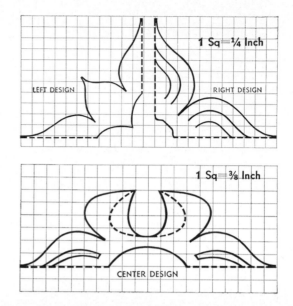

Gather ribbon scraps from Christmas gift wrapping to create the ornaments on this page. Large baubles may require a heavy-weight ribbon for pleasing results.

Loops and rings are held in position with glue or staples or by moistening the stick-to-itself type of ribbon. For color combinations, use double layers of ribbon with each a different color. Two layers also add strength.

Extras such as document seals or paper cutouts will provide color and shape accents.

After adapting these designs to your own use try creating additional, original ribbon pieces.

86

Triangle tree bagatelles can be finished in a variety of ways, but each begins with a four-inch equilateral triangle of colorful construction paper. Centers of triangle sides are marked and creased between as drawing below illustrates. Then four or five of these units are stapled together at crease lines to form three-dimensional stars. For a two-sided design, two stars are stapled together back-to-back, overlapping or alternating the points. For contrast, design can have colors alternate around the star or between the front and the back or two sides can be joined with seals.

Another variation of the basic fold is formed by leaving the points free after stapling four or five creased units together at the fold lines. This is accomplished by stapling the points together flat with adjoining unit, or by overlapping the points and stapling them together. Colors for these variations may be alternated for special interest and effect, too. For other variations, decorate the unit centers or points with seals, stars, and cutouts. Hang on the Christmas tree with fine nylon filament wire or thread.

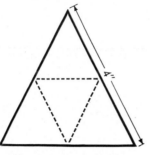

Material for trims above

Colored gift-wrapping papers Gold seals or decorative stickers Staples and stapler Glue Gummed tape

Procedure

Paper Balls:
Cut 20 paper circles of uniform size. Make a cardboard equilateral triangle with its points just touching edges of circle. Place triangle on circle, fold and crease the three visible portions to form flanges. Staple together on the creases, five flanged triangles to form bottom of ball. Repeat to form top but before stapling last two circles fix a shallow paper cone with double-faced tape (cut halfway across paper circle; overlap slightly). Place inside top to close hole where five points meet.

Thread hanging wire, ribbon, or string through cone.
Cube in three colors:
Cut six five-inch squares, two of each color. (Called A, B, C.) Fold each point to the center, forming a smaller box with the creases. Lay the squares with four in a line and three at one end forming a T shape. Join at

triangles formed by the creases. Arrange colors ABAB with the two Cs on each side of first A. Staple first A and last B together to form a box, flanges out. Staple Cs together to form top and

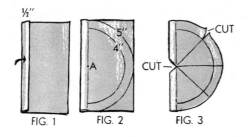

bottom of box. Fold all flanges flat over cube sides and fasten with decorative stickers. Thread wire or string through one corner and hang.

Four-sided double pyramid:

Fold a 10x11-inch paper in half, making fold on 10-inch side. Fold center fold over ½ inch (Fig. 1). Unfold ½-inch fold and mark center of paper on fold crease. Draw both a 5- and a 4-inch circle from center point (Fig. 2). Leaving paper folded, cut out half circle at 5-inch mark. Fold this in half, then in fourths, making all creases meet at center of circle (A in Fig. 2). Make one-inch cuts on creases from edge of paper to 4-inch mark. Fold flaps up. Cut wedge (Fig. 3).

Unfold and cut circle in two on center fold (in between half-inch crease). Lay semicircles together; staple three flaps at creases. Cut ½-inch flanges at center crease ½ inch; overlap flanges and staple, then glue flat on pyramids.

Top ornament for tree:

This is a combination of the ball (made from 2-inch circles) and a 7-sided double pyramid. Follow pyramid instructions but fold circle into 1/16ths.

This Parade Tree is loaded with handsome Sergeant Majors and a Sousa-like array of drums. Soldiers are built of leftover cardboard cylinders. For arms and legs, split cylinders in half, roll together and tape. Attach legs and arms with tape. Cover with felt and trim with sequins and braid. Drums can be cut from plastic foam and large mailing tubes. Cover sides with velvet and tops with felt. Add braid and rims.

Cardboard ornament on right is cut, scored, and bent following above pattern. Masking tape secures edges. Burlap glues in place to cover.

To present that "little something" in an attractive way, these stunning pyramids serve as gift paquettes and double as attractive tree trinkets.

Begin making tree and gift paquettes by enlarging patterns below. Trace patterns onto lightweight cardboard, (these are made from gold and silver cardboard). The pattern illustrations are for both three- and four-sided gift holders.

Score on the back of the cardboard along the dotted lines. While still flat, decorate the panels with construction or gift wrapping paper, fabric, jewels, sewing trim, gold lace paper, sequins, or yarn.

Punch tiny holes at top and thread with fine wire for hanging. Spread rubber cement on narrow flap of three-sided pyramid and on fifth triangle of four-sided pyramid. Apply glue also on edges that will meet. Finish by inserting gift and sealing bottom with glue.

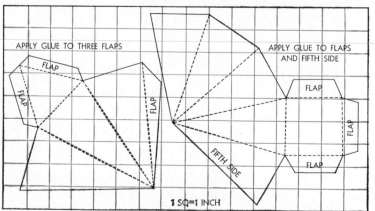

APPLY GLUE TO THREE FLAPS

FLAP

FLAP

FLAP

APPLY GLUE TO FLAPS AND FIFTH SIDE

FLAP

FLAP

FLAP

FIFTH SIDE

1 SQ = 1 INCH

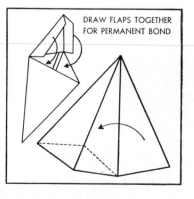

DRAW FLAPS TOGETHER FOR PERMANENT BOND

Bauble designs combine yarn, braid, bows, sequins, and beads for a contemporary effect.

Box magic! Personalized tree ornaments can come from the most likely or unlikely objects found in any house. Decorated toothpaste boxes, tissue paper cylinders, or, like the baubles on the left, just small gift boxes can become sparkling additions to the tree.

Select two boxes similar in shape and balanced in proportion for these easy-to-make ornaments. Wrap the boxes individually with foil wrapping paper, fabric, or paint them with shiny enamels. Wrap velvet ribbon around each box and add a bow at the top. Small beads attach to the bottom and sides of the bow with hatpins. String boxes together with fine wire strung through beads and then through the boxes.

Decorate tissue or wrapping paper cylinders or toothpaste boxes in the same way, but with only one section. Paint, or cover the boxes or cylinders with material. Add rickrack, gold and silver sewing trims, sequins, glass beads, hatpins, ribbon, foil paper stickers or cutouts. Attach string or braid through a hole punched in the top and hang them from the tree.

Tree Santas: They're cardboard base triangles camouflaged with paint and excelsior. Each triangle has a three-inch base and eight-inch sides. Join three triangles with tape on the inside or with glue. Spray paint the cardboard (or cover with red felt), add black felt eyes and a red Christmas ball nose. Beads glue to top section to outline hat. Glue on newspaper or wrapping excelsior for beard, mustache, and fur.

White flocking and soft blue ornaments make a quiet and peaceful combination for a Christmas tree. These decorative trinkets are made from apple dividers used in crates of apples. Cut the dividers around indented areas in pairs. Make smaller circles by cutting the full space that holds the apples. Wire or glue the smaller piece to the larger two. Attach a matching section to the back with glue making the ornament symmetrical. After the glue is dry, spray the dividers with a water base paint and add trims. These are velvet ribbon, sections from gold lace doilies, fabric remnants, and glass beads.

New apple dividers are made of plastic foam. These can be painted and glued just as the cardboard ones. Use a white glue and a water base paint. Designs can be etched into the surface of the foam with a light amount of airplane glue which dissolves the plastic or with certain kinds of paints.

Combine the ornaments with matching and adjacent colors for a pleasing, and soothing color scheme.

Glossy oilcloth lanterns reflect the lights from the Christmas tree and radiate their cheerfulness. Cut three-inch bases, and eight-inch sides for the cardboard triangles on the lower portion. Top triangles have five-inch bases and three-inch sides. Glue or tape the sections together, then glue oilcloth to the lower part. Cover the top the same or spray with paint. Connect the two sections and insert wire into the top.

Paper cups glued together and trimmed with burlap, calico, oilcloth, and tissue fringe will make attractive additions to any tree. To cover a cone with cloth, make a semicircle pattern with the radius equal to the measurement from the tip to the rim of the cup. Glue the material to the cup matching edges. Cover edges where material meets with strips of sewing trim, gold foil paper, or additional material.

Decorate the cones with anything that is available. Hang the ornaments from the tree with ribbon or thread strung through the tip.

Oilcloth in red and red and white stripes wraps around these pointed cups to create cheery tree or doorway trims. A pattern can be made simply by cutting a cup in half lengthwise and tracing around it on the cloth.

Another way to camouflage the double-paper cup forms is to glue on layers of fringed tissue paper in brilliant colors. Attach a tassel of ½-inch wide strips and as long as the cup to the bottom.

Fringe long narrow tissue strips (doubled over lengthwise for faster cutting). Apply rubber cement or white glue to the cup, then wind strips around until both cups are completely covered. Be sure to overlap the rows so that no empty spots show.

SMALL TREES

Small trees, just right for an apartment corner, a coffee or end table, or the guest bedroom, are as much a part of Christmas as their larger counterparts. The first Christmas trees were small pyramid-like structures laden with simple toys. Since, this custom has spread from Germany and developed until today we have the giant live evergreen trees twinkling with electric lights and sparkling with glass tree balls. Decorating styles vary from the pyramid to the evergreen and make Christmas that much more fun. The apple cone tree on the left has its origin in colonial times.

The small tree offers the designer a size variation. And the possibilities of decorating tiny live trees or of constructing original creations are limitless. From the colonial fruit cone to a futuristic sheet metal tree, you'll find imaginative and colorful trees in every category. One will be right for you.

As with the large trees, the small Christmas trees should complement and glorify their location. As much attention should be given to their adornments as to the other seasonal decorations.

Artificial red apples and crab apples, polished to perfection and teamed with jack pine, are picked into a cone-shaped foundation of hardware cloth filled with sphagnum moss.

Carnation and evergreen tree complements this Victorian decor. Chicken wire cone filled with oasis sits in a shallow water-filled bowl. Fir branches and flowers insert into oasis foam.

For a gift or as a tabletop tree—it serves as both. Spool tree makes a novel gift-decoration. Dismantled, it becomes a gift of an open wire or rattan mesh basket, 65 spools of sewing thread, and a ball of crochet thread. It's perfect for the seamstress.

To copy the tree, lace two rows of velvet ribbon in and out as indicated in the picture, string multicolor spools of sewing thread onto elastic thread and tie ends together to form a bracelet. Make two more bracelets, each a few spools larger than the previous one. Slip spool bracelets over basket and secure at three levels. Top inverted basket tree with a crochet thread-ball and glass-ball finial. Roll cardboard into a three-inch diameter tube for tree support. Finish design with natural greens and cotton velvet bow.

Color dominates the brilliant and innovational tree above. In addition to bringing a lift to Christmas decorating it offers a way to use up those odd scraps of sewing trim. The frame can be $2\frac{1}{2}$ feet high plastic foam or cardboard cone. Use wood dowels to support a cardboard cone, and use a ribbon spool base for either. Wind trims around the cone, attach with glue or pins. Place trims over trims to cover bare spots. Top with yarn flowers and ball fringe finial.

Cardboard boxes, eight of them in graduated sizes, it took to build the Christmas tree below. It is perfect for a holiday luncheon or supper centerpiece. Metal foil paper in gold, green, and red covers the boxes. Place the largest box on the bottom. This one measures 9½x15x2 inches. Place on a square-shape box in the center of the base and balance the additional trunk and tree boxes.

Decorate the boxes with velvet ribbon and stabilize the pyramid construction with wide velvet ribbon wrapped from the bottom to the top. For more ornamentation, add tree ornaments and attach with hatpins around the tree trunk at the trunk and tree junctions. Top with a finial.

For the best results, pick boxes that are similar in shape (rectangular or square) and that are proportioned the same. Sizes should decrease at an equal rate for the lines to be smooth and pleasing.

Matisse sparked the idea for this tree collage. A plastic foam cone has an oilcloth cover attached with white liquid cement. The wood dowel support inserts into the bottom of the plastic foam and then into a small box base made higher than the tree trunk and from wood or cardboard stabilized with a weight. Flower shapes of paper glue to hatpins piercing cone.

A small tree should be pretty from every angle; the perky flower tree below in a painted compote looks equally attractive when viewed from anywhere in the room.

Cover a plastic foam cone with paper to match color of compote or vase to be used as the base.

Use a sharp point to pierce holes through paper into the cone where the stems will be inserted.

Paper and plastic flowers plus a pompon ornament for a topper complete the flower tree.

Cardboard in strips, stapled together, make an attractive decoration for the coffee table. Begin by making a paper cone 22 inches high for the trunk.

Using paper strips 1⅛-inch wide, cut three green lengths for every inch size between and including 4 and 11 inches. Cut matching blue pieces plus three pieces three inches long. Form triangles by stapling three equal pieces one inch from ends. Stack the triangles on the paper cone resting a green directly on a blue with the points even, or alternating.

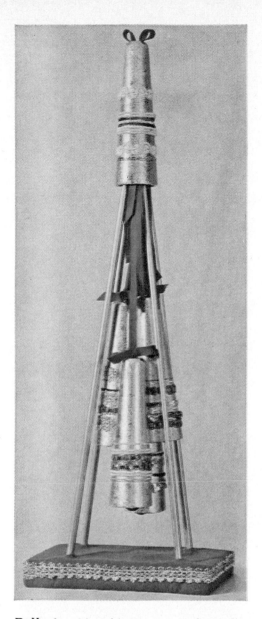

Bells for this table tree come from discarded cardboard cones of large commercial yarn, string, thread holders. Similar ones may be made by rolling cardboard. Gold foil wrapped around the cones has bottom edge tucked inside bells.

Thin copper wire sews together cut-to-size braid ends. Braid slips over bell top. Discarded bangle bracelet cut-to-size come next, followed by pearls strung on wire. Felt ribbons fastened to fine wire go through bell tops. To other end of wire fasten baubles for bell clappers. Bought in sets of four, upright 36-inch metal table legs form basic structure of tree. U-shaped metal feet on legs gives natural slant when screwed into velvet-covered wooden block base. Gathered together, felt ribbons of four bells secure in fifth bell center, then wedges over rod tops.

Sunshine colors of tissue paper give a fiesta look to Christmas. To make the tree, open tissue paper sheets to full length. Take a corner in each hand, shirr with fingers. Bring two ends together, fasten with pipe cleaner. Repeat, making layers gradually smaller. Use a one-inch diameter dowel for support. Top with gold ball.

Table tree in a Spanish mood accents other foreign decor of this room. The tree has a plastic foam cone base covered by green velour paper.

Heavy black cotton lace in the three-inch width is shirred around the bottom of the cone tree, half way up, and at the top. Then six ready-made paper roses are attached with glue on the lace at the base of the tree. Four more roses nestle in the center lace row and a cluster of five roses trims the top of the tree. The table arrangement is completed by the green and red wrapped packages placed to the left of the tree and trimmed with the same black Spanish lace and red artificial roses.

Gold paint sprayed over the sculptured tree below provides a striking background for the green glass adornments. The tree shape comes from a plastic foam cone 30 inches tall. A coat of lightweight sculpturing plaster (comes in a powder form and mixes with water to a working consistency) covers the cone. When the medium dries, the cone is sprayed gold.

A dowel stick tree trunk $\frac{5}{8}$ inch in diameter inserts into a jar and is held erect with a plaster of paris mold. Glass chips glue around the top rim of the gold sprayed jar base.

The green rings on the tree are made by firing green bottle necks in a kiln at about 450° until softened, curling, and gluing on tree after glass has cooled. Tiny glass chips glue among rings. Sprinkled with glitter, the plastic foam star on the top of the tree has a tiny piece of melted glass glued on with white glue.

Evergreen branches attached to a cone-shape frame and enclosed in four cardboard triangles sits on top of a piano for the conical tree at the left. Tall triangles are covered with green and blue foil paper. A string of small Christmas balls falls along the edges outlining the triangles from top to the bottom.

Foil poinsettias lie at the base of the triangles. More small blue balls decorate the flower centers. A commercial star adorned with green ribbon sits on top of the tree. Gifts, wrapped to match, complete the grouping.

Slash copper on lines from cone tip to dotted line; curl tips. Cut away seam allowance shown as shaded area. Overlap cone to dotted line, glue to secure. Do not texture seam allowance underlap, tree tip. Make narrow aluminum foil tabs by folding three or four times. Press them over goblet rim to secure shades upon.

Copper trees at right stand on copper painted glass goblets. To make trees, spray goblet stems, lower part of bowl with copper paint. Roll paper into cone to create patterns. Allow one-inch overlap at bottom for seam. Trace pattern onto copper sheet, cut out. Lay copper flat on newspaper pad, texture underside by hammering with ball peen hammer. Leave top notch of tree, underlap of seam allowance untextured. Tap gently around edges with flat side of hammer to reduce curl. Turn piece over, burnish top with fine steel wool. Antique, rinse in clean water, dry. Place top side down on newspaper pad, pierce textured areas with small nail. Slash tree tip as directed in drawing above, cut away seam allowance of tree tip on one side. Curl tips out slightly.

Roll copper into cone, overlapping edges smoothly. Spread thin layer of epoxy on seam underlap. Tie until glue sets. Glue balls on tips.

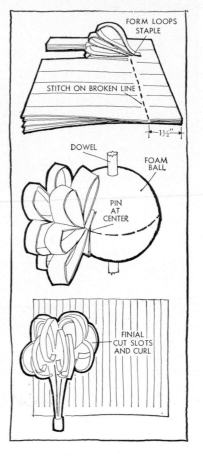

Opulent is the word for the table tree at the right, fashioned of loops of heavy crepe paper in shades of lime and holiday green.

To begin, spray a three-inch, a 2½-inch, a two-inch foam ball, and a 32-inch dowel (pointed at the top) all green. Thread balls on the dowel and set into a food-container base which has been covered with paper and sprayed gold. The dowel is anchored in a lump of florists' clay inside the container.

Stack four 9x10-inch pieces of heavy crepe paper (cut on crossgrain). Use double thickness if lighter weight crepe is used. Sew or staple 1½ inches from 10-inch edge. Cut wider part into one-inch strips up to the stitches or staples.

Loop each strip back as shown in the diagram above; staple strip to itself. Pin loops around the three-inch ball. Repeat for the other two tiers from paper cut 9x7½ inches for the 2½-inch ball and 8x6 inches for the 2-inch ball. Cut the strips smaller for correct proportion.

Curl the strips for the top and glue them around the dowel below a finial. Stick red berries and white fruit (real or artificial) into foam balls between the loops.

Dressmaker tree, left, utilizes all those leftover bits of braid, binding, rickrack, yarn, and pompons. Gather all the "edgings" into full rosettes and center with more trims. On a plastic foam cone sprayed green, arrange and pin the flowers in a pleasing pattern.

Woodcraft tree form can be made with cedar triangles. Make three triangles with the sides of 14, 20, and 25 inches. Rub off-white paint into the wood for an antiqued effect. Drill holes through wood to insert a long brass rod and glue in place. Drill another hole into a rough log and set the rod into the base.

Coiled straw purchased at a millinery supply house creates this unique tree. The coils are secured onto a florist cone with long straight pins. Uniformly sized coils placed close together form the first tree layer. The second layer has irregular sized coils forming "S" shapes that cover the gaps between the coils of the first layer. Finish with green foliage.

Individual pine cone segments create this version of the traditional Christmas tree. The plastic foam, 16-inches high cone foundation has a green ceramic candlestick pedestal purchased at the dime store. A two-inch deep plug cut from the bottom of the cone fits to the three-inch candle stub in the candlestick, supporting the cone. For ease of handling, the attachment is completed first, dismantled to decorate the cone, then reassembled.

To decorate, spray the cone gold. Encircle cone base with ½-inch wide green satin rope, continue circling the tree to the top. Indicate placement on cone with felt-tipped pen after pinning the rope in place. Remove rope.

Clipping close to stem, remove scales from large pine cones with a flower arranger's long pointed shears. Protect hands with gloves. Coat plastic foam cone with resin glue, place "petals" on in overlapping rows, following the spiral rope pattern. Begin at base with largest petals, using smaller petals toward top. Leave marked areas open. Finish design by covering marked areas with resin glue, placing rope in position. Top tree with flower cone made from a slice from a small cone base.

Ticker tape combines with ornaments and coins for the "Wall Street Christmas Tree" on the right. Stuff ticker tape, transparent and solid, into a chicken wire cone allowing a few streamers to fall casually onto the table. (Protect table surface with a cloth circle.) Insert Christmas tree ball ornaments into the wire and attach coins with tape or glue to provide color and to complete the businessman's Christmas tree.

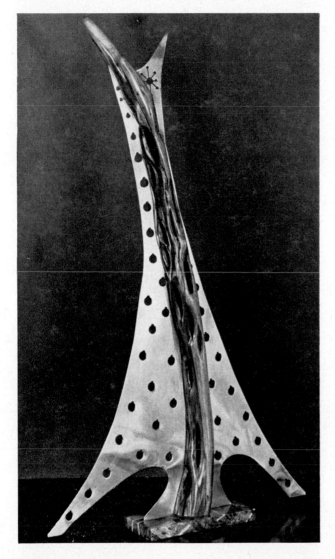

Futuristic tree below uses 60 pieces of 24-inch long, 12-gauge wire. Secure wires together at several points. Solder bottom ends together, keeping shape round. Cut ½-inch thick plywood disk base in desired diameter. Next, cut two smaller disks, drill holes in centers to hold wire tree shaft, glue in place. Spray paint entire base. Bend wire branches down from shaft, eight to a tier. Wire to hold. Glue on paper circles, concave triangles.

Driftwood collectors can use their finds for their Christmas decorating. Remove the bark from a fairly straight piece of driftwood. Sand the wood until it is completely smooth. Apply two coats of Danish stain and sand after each coat. Cut two pieces of ⅛-inch brass into free-form tree halves; fit them into grooves running lengthwise in the wood. With a metal drill, make holes and a starburst into the brass. File the tree smooth to finish and place into sanded rectangle base.

BUFFET AND TABLE ARRANGEMENTS

Flat surfaces of tabletops, buffets, stereos, and dressers invite bright, colorful, and even whimsical holiday adornments. What a perfect place to let your fancy roam! And what a perfect place to establish and carry out a theme. Select one item to use as the basis for every table topper, then design arrangements for the television, end table, dining table, kitchen counter, and telephone stand. Simplicity should be the key.

These table toppers can become distinctive decorative items; they're made from nondescript materials such as mailing tubes, tin cans, or cotton. With the aid of cloth, paper, and glue they become candles, bells, and snowmen set into a wintry scene with evergreens.

White faience bowl holds low arrangement of spruce, holly, and bright artificial berries for welcoming decoration at left. Backed by tall candles, decoration suits entry or dining area.

Simulated beeswax candles form focal point of arrangement below. Cover cardboard tubes with beeswax sheets; join edges by pressing. Add pine cones and persimmons to long needle pine.

This attractive arrangement for a table or buffet top has for its components the top halves of champagne bottles, velvet ribbon, and apples. To create a similar decoration, cut an ellipsoidal shape from the center of a plastic foam rectangle measuring 8x12x2 inches. Place the cutout piece on top of one end of the remaining plastic foam frame for a platform.

Have the bottle necks removed by a profes-

sional glass cutter and line cut edge with lead. Push necks into foam. Secure tall candles into position using small mounds of floral clay.

Pin spruce tips or other greens into the base creating an asymmetrical arrangement. Nestle red velvet bows and hand-polished apples among the greens in the center of the grouping. Make feathers by placing wire between two lengths of ribbon and gluing them together

Champagne bottle bottoms appear as candle holders in the Christmas-red arrangement below. The bottle necks are removed and used for the holders across the page. Seal the edges with lead. The base of the display is plastic foam wrapped with red velvet. Three smaller pieces of foam with varying thicknesses are covered to match. Into these are inserted the rims of the inverted bottles, allowing the candles to stand at different levels.

Floral clay adheres bits of foam in the cupped bottle bottoms. Floral clay holds the candles, also. Red velvet bows and small artificial berries pin into the foam bits at the bottom of the candles and around the bottle bases. Sprigs of glittered, artificial leaves arrange around the bottles to complete the design.

Evergreen and bottle swag graces a wall above a patio table. The lighted arrangement uses five bottles—three long and two round shapes of different sizes. Wide neck bottles are most suitable for inserting strings of tiny Italian lights.

To make a basket for holding bottles, clip in half a fine wire measuring seven times the length of the bottle being used. Twist pieces together in the center and tape centers to outside bottom of bottle. Wind one wire from each side to the opposite wire. Twist original wires together and continue alternating and twisting wires at equal intervals up the bottle until a basket-like webbing is created. When the top of the bottle is reached, tie the extending pieces of wire around a long, narrow sheet of green plastic foam securing tightly with tacks or pins. Remove the tape from the bottom bottle.

Wire evergreen branches to the foam. Center with clusters of red silk balls. Set off greens with a three-inch-wide velvet bow and streamers. Wire remaining bottles in place after filling with Italian lights. Conceal wires with more bows and ribbon.

Stair-stepped candles grouped on an end table before cascading salal leaves give a Christmas glow to holiday decorating. Cardboard mailing tubes are covered with gold paper placemats cut to size. Sets from unused jewelry are mounted with glue to accent the lacy pattern of the paper. Votive candles in colors that harmonize with the room are set into top.

Groups of three or five candles would look equally as attractive as an end table arrangement.

The beauty of stained glass can be created by an amateur with the help of textured shower door glass. Cut ¼-inch wood dowels into lengths ranging from 12 to 24 inches. Sharpen one end to a point; flatten one side with sandpaper and paint them green. Cut shower glass into triangles. Coat textured side with transparent glass paint available in hobby stores. Adhere flat side of dowels to glass with epoxy glue. Arrange in plastic foam with evergreens and candles into an attractive grouping.

Surprise holiday dinner guests with this sleek centerpiece running the full length of the table. Have the bottle necks from five matching bottles removed. Save the bottom portions and edge the rims with lead. Next, cut a long narrow sheet of plastic foam for a base, cover it with green paper, and adhere the bottles to the foam in three heights with floral clay.

Partially fill each bottle with instant candle wax (comes in granule form). Center each with the wick which is included in the instant wax package. Completely cover the base with spruce sprigs, gold painted walnuts, white florets, and green velvet bows.

A candle variety group in colorful clear glass pieces makes a smart addition to that special table or buffet. Almost any lovely colored glass piece will do that will hold the instant candle wax granules. Purchase attractive containers from a florist or florist supply house, or use pieces you already have. Fill the containers with the wax granules (they come in a variety of colors, too). Insert the wick that comes with the wax and you're ready to arrange your own attractive table or buffet group. The candle granules can be purchased at the florist shop, also.

Make your own candles for holiday decorating with melted paraffin (for candles). The precious jade-like squares above are made in milk cartons filled with ice cubes. Pour in warm wax, let it cool, then unmold draining off water.

Inexpensive glasses at the left are filled with wax and wicks, glued together and trimmed with fringe and ribbon. Burn one and then reverse to other side like an hourglass!

Co-ordinated candles highlight the Christmas pudding. Create candles in kitchen molds; place on tray (bottom left).

Layered barber-pole candles below using colored paraffin leftovers, were molded in frozen food containers.

Wise Men bottles sit atop this table. Three tall matching bottles form the basic shapes. The bottles sit in gold poster board bases made in three heights. Gold paper forms crowns, necks, and hands, also. Acetate in three colors attaches to the necks for the capes and decorates the crowns. The heads and two gifts are glass floats decorated with small glass jewels and beads. Sequins, pearls, beads, and paper decorate gold paper sleeves and crowns. Fringed foil decorates neck.

Pattern a Christmas table after a pretty party napkin like the ones above. The green and gold design on the napkins is repeated in the puffs made of two inch circles of gold Japanese tea paper set on 3½-inch circles of green tissue paper. Long florist pins hold the puffs on plastic foam balls. The puffs sit in small salt dishes. Twisted and pinched gold and green circles on curled pipe cleaners are placed by napkins for individual favors.

Christmas centerpiece of three small bowls sits on this family room table. Dampened squares of plastic foam or florists' moss rest in the bottoms of the antique bowls. Small branches with red berries insert into the foam. A large candle centers on the table with a gold sunburst Christmas ornament on the top. This easy-to-assemble yuletide centerpiece is attractive and convenient—it can go almost anywhere.

To continue the color theme, cut a red felt tablecloth to fit your table. Hunt, or make napkins in a green to match the green leaves of the sprigs in the bowls.

Velvet ribbon provides a wonderful way to coordinate Christmas decorating. Chartreuse velvet florist ribbon accents wall, individual favors, length of table, and packages in setting at right.

Swags of preserved pine branches, stems masked together with tape, are sprayed white and hung in the center of the wall ribbons. Simulated crystal drops from a lighting supply house wire into the swags to catch the light. Favor boxes have ribbon loops showing both sides of the ribbon and are held by gold pins.

Simple but impressive ornaments were made by pinning gold metallic leaves around plastic foam balls, threading gold beads onto long gold hatpins, and sticking them into the balls through leaves. Artificial gold leaves fill spaces between pins and beads so that a solid gold effect is achieved.

The centerpiece at the left shows off a collection of vibrant red and pink roses and clear gossamer teardrop tree ornaments. The clear glass baubles are carefully secured at the ends of balloon sticks with wire, then set among the flower blooms in a pleasing pattern. A glittery runner of silver and white creates a sumptuous look. Arrangement colors complement the magentas of the tablecloth and china place settings.

Christmas Eve dessert table setting mirrors warmth and charm with its traditional colors of red and green, accented by snowy white. The centerpiece is of natural cypress green cascading from a gold bowl. Red and gold glass ball ornament accents in a variety of sizes attach to the green foliage and rest in the bowl.

Pine cone candleholder is made by removing the tip from a giant cone and inserting a screw-in holder. Evergreens and gold figures on the window seat continue the color theme.

The cherry red poinsettia has its own special way of saying "Merry Christmas." Use several plants throughout the house for a traditional red and green holiday celebration. At the right we show chemically dwarfed poinsettias in gilded pots forming the low centerpiece for this crimson and gold holiday table. Two crimson runners travel the length of the table topped with the flowers and candles. A corsage made from a single blossom awaits each lady guest. Small poinsettia plants may be bought at florists, nurseries, or variety stores.

Holiday table setting can often be skillfully produced with the simplest of ingredients. This centerpiece consists of a candle, held by florist clay, burning in a hurricane shade. Its foot is completely covered by an arrangement of magnolia leaves gold sprayed, red persimmons, blackberries, and lightly sprayed succulent plants. The arrangement was made on an aluminum foil base, then set in place.

Christmas roses bloom with wild profusion on an exquisite holiday table, echoing the subtle, striped wall covering and burnished copper paint tones.

Roses are secured on a plastic base by florists' wire prongs, interspersed with glittering gold tree ornaments. More of the satin-tone roses are arranged down length of the table surrounding two tall green taper candles.

Try clusters made into individual corsages, centered as we have done on a square folded napkin. The flowers can be made or bought. Colors available make it easy to pick up scheme of dining room.

Cherished Italian pewter tureen becomes focal point for this festive table setting. Lustrous tureen contains a water-saturated plastic foam material used in flower arranging. Lid of container presses into foam to hold.

English holly kept fresh in moistened foam and chopstick-skewered apples are positioned on each side of the lid. Slits in top of plastic apples spray-painted with pewter paint, hold place cards (paint dries in about one week).

Traditional oyster stew on Christmas Eve looks twice as appetizing in this attractive setting. Smart plastic placemats of forest green, and deep blue goblets and napkins (in a necktie knot), are the colorful props for the white bowls and green-banded plates.

In matching blue and green hues, patio candles placed in center of table gleam like tree balls nestled in evergreen and holly. Evergreen sprigs lace in and out of the candles and run the length of the dining table.

An apple tree is a pleasing sight for a Christmastime brunch. Evergreen branches, red carnations, and apples combine to make the table-piece design. The tree is easily made by forming a chicken wire cone base, then wiring the evergreens, apples, and carnations in place. Wire cone secures on a glass compote spray painted with gold paint.

The compote, resting on a dampened plastic foam chunk, is surrounded by more natural greens and leaves of holly. Red spiraled candles rest in brass candlesticks on each side of the tree. Reds and greens appear again in tablecloth and napkins, also in the matching plates, cups, and saucers.

Tiny Tim Buffet—plenty of spirit here on the copper-lined replica of an old-fashioned dry sink on the right. The sink doubles as a buffet for serving holiday supper guests.

Decorations remain simple because of an abundance of food. Small imitation trees and red candles in copper holders trace sides of the buffet.

Candy centerpiece is good enough to eat and that's what it is for! Candelabrum is an inverted ceiling fixture resting on an antique turkey platter deep enough to hold water for greens and carnations. Marzipan fruits, candy secure with hooks.

Doughnut tree, just made to be eaten, stands 36 inches high, has a wood dowel shaft with a one-inch diameter. Tree arms are dowels ⅜ inch in diameter. The tree frame is painted and placed in a papier mache bait bucket. Green burlap covers the outside of bucket and cardboard base in which it sits. Popcorn fills the inside of each. Red cotton upholstery braid adds a colorful accent to the bucket. The tree holds about nine dozen large doughnuts.

Boy and girl trees holding cookies and pretzels have metal frames. Stands are made of number two cans covered with felt, set in pie plates decorated with braid around the edges. Trees stand 24-inches high with 14-inch arm spreads. Legs of boy slip off center metal pin for loading with pretzels. Candy lemon slices make his ears, a paper cup his hat.

Toothpicks inserted in holes drilled in center shaft hold pretzels which form girl's skirt. Gumdrops hold the pretzels on the picks. Corn curls form hair and glue to the giant sucker head. A green felt bow perches on top of her hair.

Fasten satin streamers to the ceiling above your Christmas breakfast table with masking tape, or a tack for a tile ceiling, then to four points on the table. Suspend a paper flower bouquet in the center; tack four more onto the satin streamers where streamers meet the table. Add bows and streamers to center bouquet and to table points.

Make flowers by folding five-inch-wide strip of tissue paper in half; wind to rose shape.

Small food cans covered with colored tissue paper form the pyramid fixture suspended above the table pictured below. Cans hang from three wire hoops spray-painted orange. The hoops are graduated in sizes to create a tree effect. Small yarn balls are connected to the bottoms of each can. Cans hang by yarn in a color to match the hoops. A large knot is tied in one end of the yarn. The other end is strung through the can bottom from the inside and tied to the hoops. Yarn balls tie to knot on the inside of the cans.

Yardage cut in circular shape makes tablecloth. Tree on table is spray-painted cardboard triangle.

Table trimming hangs overhead instead of on the table. A plastic salad bowl is suspended like a balloon gondola, heaped with small surprises to finish the feast. Paint the bowl a brilliant hue, then paste on seals and metallic paper stars.

124

Snowman merry-go-round will start holiday meals off right! To make the merry-go-round, cut sides of a 14-inch diameter hat box 3½-inches high; turn upside down. Cut 16-inch diameter cardboard circle; slash from edge to direct center.

Beginning at slash, tape circle edge to hatbox lid to form roof. As you tape last part of circle to box, it will overlap to form peak. Cover base and roof with wrapping paper. Cut 2½-inch wide band into six points, tape around edge of roof. Decorate with gold tape.

Snowmen are seven 8-inch tubes covered with wrapping paper. Wrap 4-inch area of tubes with cotton; tie with ribbon to form neck. Cut 4-inch paper circle hat brims; cut circles out of centers to fit over tubes. Add star eyes, ball nose, ribbon hatband to each. Tape tube in base center, snowmen around edge.

Madras striped tissue in blues and greens creates a variety of eye-catching decorations for a New Year's Eve party. Make pompons used as basis for all decorations at the right by cutting a six-inch-wide strip of tissue across length of one sheet. Fold strip in half lengthwise (width will be three inches), creasing fold tightly. Then fold accordion style into 3x7½-inch rectangles. Cut deep scallops along open edge to within one inch of folded edge. Unfold. Gather through the center with thread and secure with cotton-covered spool wire. Wrap 6½-inch length of white cotton covered spool wire with tinsel. Attach to center of pompon.

For wreath, form a ring of heavy cotton covered wire or lightweight coat hanger. Attach pompons to the ring so scallops overlap. If used as we have to encircle a punch bowl, one row will suffice. If wreath is to hang where both sides will be seen, add more pompons. Hang single pompons from ceiling. Cut smaller pompons to tie around napkins and to decorate packages.

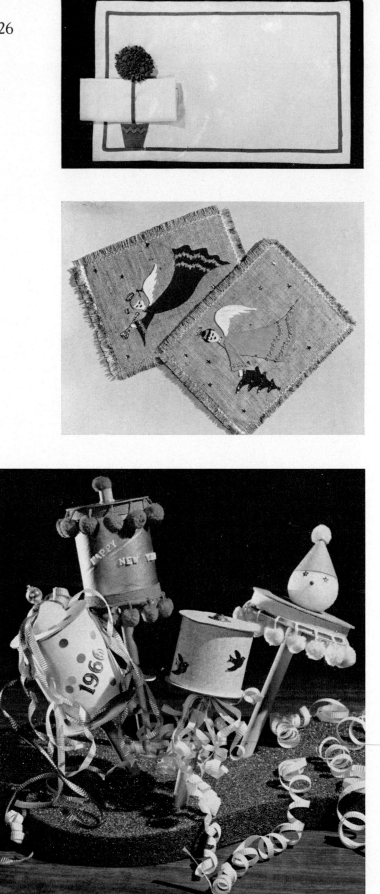

Make cheery topiary tree placemats for a special Christmas breakfast this season, then you'll have them to use for several Christmas parties to come. Mat is decorated with a green bias tape border, wide hem tape tree base, bias tape trunk, and rickrack tree top.

Christmas placemats can easily convert to wall hangings. These are made by fringing burlap rectangles, bordering with rickrack, then decorating centers with felt and rickrack angels and sequin stars.

Convert mats to wall hangings by inserting corrugated paper between mat and second layer of fringed burlap. Then attach a twine hanger to the back and you're ready to perk up a Christmas wall.

A New Year's party wouldn't be complete without noisemakers and these double as a snappy centerpiece set in a spray-painted plastic foam base.

Noisemakers can be constructed in two ways. One way is to place small rocks or bells in an empty ribbon spool, insert a wooden dowel handle, and glue it to secure. Spray-paint and trim, then spell out a New Year's greeting with alphabet macaroni.

The other way is to paint the dowel handles separately. While they dry, cover the ends and sides of the spools with construction paper and adhesive film. Place the noisemaking material inside the spools, insert the handles, and glue. Decorate with sequins, embossed letters, colored dots, sewing trims, glass baubles, and curled ribbon streamers.

Dry beans, peas, macaroni, or popcorn can fill the noisemakers. Tacks or BBs will also give a different sound.

Lighthearted companions of Christmas stand out on pure white breakfast bar and help spread Christmas to every room in the house. Jovial felt Santa, pinked and pocketed, locates place setting, under the watchful eye of a lively stuffed deer. Glue felt placemat parts, beard, belt, hat, and face to red oval body. Stitch on the pocket before adding the belt. Add eyes and brows with a marking pen.

A lamp chimney with a felt face and cap is filled with mints. A wooden sleigh filled with miniature gifts and goodies and green ivy leaves continues the theme.

Vigil-light candles in little red and white hobnail cups add a pleasing sparkle to this vibrant holiday arrangement—placed low to encourage cross-table conversation. Green placemats with machine-stitched Yuletide tree ornament patterns make a festive foil for milkglass dinnerware and ruby crystal fruit dishes. Similar mats can be made of colorful paper with crayon designs drawn on free hand.

HOLIDAY FOODS

You'll catch the spirit of Christmas easily and quickly with one whiff of mouth-watering Chocolate Pretzel Cookies, spiced hot Wassail, Christmas Fruit Balls, or Kris Kringle Cake. Christmas wouldn't seem like Christmas without the traditions that enrich it; certain Christmas delicacies are definitely a yuletide tradition and here to stay. As a gift, holiday foods are suitable for anyone, and welcome, too! Fruitcakes are ideal for mailing; cookies are definite hits with kids; fancy breads from foreign lands go great with grandmothers. Food gifts never reach a limit and are everyone's favorites. And, of course, holiday entertaining would not be the same without the holiday treats. Serving your specialties to holiday guests gives true pleasure to yuletide festivities.

Treats from your kitchen

Any of these gift ideas in bright Christmas wrap are sure to please. At left: Chocolate Pretzel Cookies, Poinsettia Petal Cookies, festive cranberry pie, and Frosty Lemon Fluff Pie. At right: White Cake Supreme with Fluffy Frosting decorated for the holidays with peppermint drops and candy canes. Pretty jellies make any meal merrier, and Christmas Fruit Balls and Easy Butter Crunch are great for snacking!

WHITE CAKE SUPREME

¾ cup shortening
1½ cups sugar
1½ teaspoons vanilla
2¼ cups sifted cake flour
3 teaspoons baking powder
1 teaspoon salt
1 cup skim milk
5 stiff-beaten egg whites

Cream shortening and sugar together until light and fluffy (beat about 10 minutes at medium-high speed on electric mixer, scraping bowl occasionally to guide batter into beaters). Add vanilla and mix well.

Sift flour with baking powder and salt; add to creamed mixture alternately with milk, beating after each addition. Fold in egg whites. Bake in 2 greased and lightly floured 9x1½-inch round cake pans in moderate oven (375°) for 18 to 20 minutes. Cool. Frost with Fluffy Frosting given below and decorate with peppermint drops and candy canes to match picture.

FLUFFY FROSTING

1 cup sugar
¼ teaspoon cream of tartar
Dash salt
⅓ cup water
2 egg whites
1 teaspoon vanilla

Bring sugar, cream of tartar, salt, and water to boiling; cook until sugar dissolves. Add *very slowly* to unbeaten egg whites, beating constantly with electric mixer till stiff peaks form. Add vanilla. Frosts tops and sides of two 8- or 9-inch cake layers or one 10-inch tube cake.

POINSETTIA PETAL COOKIES

½ cup shortening
¼ cup brown sugar
1 egg yolk
1 tablespoon lemon juice
½ teaspoon vanilla
1 cup sifted all-purpose flour
½ teaspoon salt
1 slightly beaten egg white
½ cup finely chopped
   California walnuts
Candied cherries, cut in eighths

Cream shortening and sugar. Beat in egg yolk, lemon juice, and vanilla. Sift flour and salt together; stir into mixture; chill 1 hour.

Form into 1-inch balls; dip in egg white and roll in nuts. Place on cookie sheet and top each with 3 cherry pieces arranged as petals. Bake at 350° for 18 minutes. Let stand a few minutes before removing from cookie sheet. If desired, wrap tightly and freeze. Makes 20 cookies.

FROSTY LEMON FLUFF PIE

1¼ cups graham-cracker crumbs
¼ cup sugar
6 tablespoons butter or margarine, melted
2 egg yolks
2 tablespoons sugar
3 tablespoons lemon juice
1½ teaspoons grated lemon peel
¼ teaspoon salt
½ cup whipping cream, whipped
2 egg whites
¼ cup sugar
Green gumdrops
Red cinnamon candies

Combine first 3 ingredients; press firmly into 9-inch pie plate. Chill. Beat egg yolks; gradually add 2 tablespoons sugar; beat till thick and lemon-colored. Stir in lemon juice, peel, and salt. Fold in whipped cream. Beat egg whites till soft peaks form; gradually add ¼ cup sugar, beating till stiff peaks form; fold into lemon mixture. Spoon into crumb crust; freeze firm.

Roll gumdrops on a sugared board to flatten; arrange on top of pie in shape of Christmas tree. Place cinnamon candies at ends of branches.

LIGHT FRUITCAKE

½ pound (1 cup) candied pineapple, chopped
¼ pound (½ cup) chopped mixed candied fruits and peels
¾ pound (1½ cups) candied cherries, chopped
¼ pound (½ cup) candied lemon peel
¼ pound (½ cup) candied orange peel, chopped
1 cup light raisins
1 cup California walnuts, chopped
3 cups sifted all-purpose flour
1 cup butter or margarine
1 cup sugar
4 eggs
¼ cup light corn syrup
¼ cup orange juice
¼ cup sherry

Combine chopped pineapple, mixed fruits and peels, cherries, lemon peel, orange peel, raisins, and chopped walnuts; dredge well with 1 cup of the sifted flour. Cream butter and sugar together till light and fluffy. Add eggs, one at a time, beating well after each addition. Combine corn syrup, orange juice, and sherry; add alternately with remaining 2 cups flour to creamed mixture. Fold in fruits and nuts. Pour into two well-greased 5½-cup ring molds. Bake in a very slow oven (275°) for 1 hour 15 minutes. Makes two 2-pound 4-ounce cakes.

Or, pour batter into foil muffin cups, using ¼ cup batter for each cup. Bake at 275° for about 45 minutes. Makes about 2½ dozen.

PUDDING HARD SAUCE

2 tablespoons hot water
½ cup softened butter
3 cups sifted confectioners' sugar
1 teaspoon vanilla or rum extract
½ cup chopped California walnuts
¼ cup chopped candied cherries

Blend hot water and butter; gradually add the sugar, beating till fluffy. Stir in remaining ingredients. Drop by teaspoons on waxed paper and chill. Use to trim Regal Plum Pudding.

To flame pudding: dip a sugar cube in lemon extract or any flavoring with a high alcoholic content. Place cube on top of the pudding. Light the sugar cube immediately and carry the flaming pudding to the table.

REGAL PLUM PUDDING

4 slices bread, torn
1 cup milk
2 slightly beaten eggs
1 cup brown sugar
¼ cup orange juice
6 ounces finely chopped beef suet
1 teaspoon vanilla
2 cups raisins
1 cup dates, cut up
½ cup chopped mixed candied fruits and peels
½ cup broken California walnuts
1 cup sifted all-purpose flour
1 teaspoon soda
½ teaspoon salt
2 teaspoons cinnamon
1 teaspoon *each* mace and cloves

Soak bread in milk; beat. Stir in next 5 ingredients. Combine remaining ingredients; mix. Stir in bread mixture. Pour into well-greased 2-quart mold; tie on foil cap tightly. Place on rack in deep kettle; add boiling water to 1 inch. Cover; steam over low heat 3½ hours adding water if needed. Cool 10 minutes; unmold. Serve warm with Hard Sauce. Serves 12.

To store fruitcakes, cool in pans; turn out. Wrap in cheesecloth and moisten with brandy or wine. Wrap in foil. Store in cool place for 3 to 4 weeks, moisten once a week.

To trim, brush with hot corn syrup and decorate with nuts, candied cherries, or marzipan fruits. When set, brush again with hot syrup. Allow to dry before wrapping.

KRIS KRINGLE CAKE

Combine one 2-layer-size package spice cake mix, ¼ cup shortening, and ½ cup boiling water in large bowl. Mix till well moistened; let stand 30 minutes.

Mix at medium speed on electric mixer 2 minutes, scraping bowl constantly. Add 2 eggs, and ¼ cup sherry; beat 2 more minutes. Combine 3½ cups mixed chopped candied fruits and peels, 2 cups broken California walnuts, and 1 cup raisins; stir into cake batter.

Pour into greased and paper-lined 10-inch tube pan and bake in slow oven (300°) about 2 hours and 20 minutes or till toothpick inserted in cake comes out clean. Cool; remove from pan. Makes about 3¼ pounds.

Holiday recipes with a delicious history— Light Fruitcake Ring, Dark Fruitcake, and Regal Plum Pudding with Pudding Hard Sauce.

DARK FRUITCAKE

Combine one 6-ounce can frozen orange juice concentrate, thawed, with ½ cup molasses and one 15-ounce package (3 cups) raisins in saucepan. Bring mixture to a boil over medium heat; stir occasionally. Reduce heat; simmer 5 minutes. Remove from heat. Stir in one 1-pound jar (2 cups) mixed chopped candied fruits and peels.

Cream ½ cup butter and ⅔ cup sugar. Blend in 3 eggs, one at a time. Sift together 1¼ cups sifted all-purpose flour, ⅛ teaspoon soda, 1 teaspoon cinnamon, ½ teaspoon nutmeg, and ¼ teaspoon *each* allspice and cloves. Stir into creamed mixture. Stir in fruit mixture and ½ cup chopped California walnuts; mix to coat fruit.

Line five 5½x3x2¼-inch pans with heavy paper, allowing ½ inch to extend above all sides. Pour batter into pans, filling about ¾ full. Bake at 275° about 1½ to 1¾ hours or till done. Cool cakes in pans; remove. Wrap in foil or clear plastic wrap; store in cool place several weeks. Trim with whole almonds. Makes about 3½ pounds.

HOT SPICED WASSAIL

    6 inches stick cinnamon
    16 whole cloves
    1 teaspoon whole allspice
    3 medium-sized oranges
    Whole cloves
    6 cups apple juice *or* cider
    2 cups cranberry-juice cocktail
    ¼ cup sugar
    1 teaspoon aromatic bitters
    1 cup rum

Break stick cinnamon in pieces; tie in a cheese-cloth bag with 16 cloves and whole allspice. Stud oranges with whole cloves.

    In saucepan, combine apple juice, cranberry-juice cocktail, sugar, and aromatic bitters. Add bag of spices and oranges; simmer, covered, 10 minutes. Stir in rum and heat through. Remove spices and oranges. Pour into warm serving bowl and float oranges atop. Makes 9 cups.

SWEDISH FRUIT SOUP

Start a tradition for loved ones with this delicious holiday dessert. Or for a hostess gift, present recipe and ingredients in a lovely Scandinavian bowl—

    1 11-ounce package (1¾ cups)
       mixed dried fruits
    ½ cup light raisins
    3 to 4 inches stick cinnamon
    4 cups water
    1 medium orange, unpared, cut in
       ¼-inch slices
    1 1-pint 2-ounce can (2¼ cups) un-
       sweetened pineapple juice
    ½ cup currant jelly
    ¼ cup sugar
    2 tablespoons quick-cooking tapioca
    ¼ teaspoon salt

Combine mixed dried fruits, raisins, cinnamon, and water. Bring to boiling, then simmer uncovered till fruits are tender, about 30 minutes.

    Add remaining ingredients. Bring to boiling; cover and cook over low heat 15 minutes longer, stirring occasionally. Serve warm or chilled. Makes 8 to 10 servings.

"Love and joy come to you and to your wassail too." This is the age-old holiday wish for special friends who gather around a bowl of fragrant Hot Spiced Wassail.

Butter a slice of German Stollen while it's still warm. Then enjoy the blend of cardamom and fruit in this tender loaf. It's wunderbar!

GERMAN STOLLEN

1 package active dry yeast
1 cup milk, scalded
½ cup butter or margarine
¼ cup sugar
1 teaspoon salt
¼ teaspoon ground cardamom
4 to 4½ cups sifted all-purpose flour
1 slightly beaten egg
1 cup raisins
¼ cup currants
¼ cup chopped mixed candied fruits
2 tablespoons grated orange peel
1 tablespoon grated lemon peel
¼ cup chopped almonds

Soften yeast in ¼ cup *warm* water. Combine hot milk, butter, sugar, salt, and cardamom; cool to lukewarm. Stir in *2 cups* of the flour; beat well. Add yeast and egg; beat well. Stir in fruits, peels and nuts. Add enough remaining flour to make soft dough. Turn out on lightly floured surface. Knead till smooth and elastic, 8 to 10 minutes. Place in greased bowl turning once to grease surface. Cover; let rise till double in a warm place, about 1 hour and 45 minutes.

Punch down; turn out on lightly floured surface; divide in 3 equal parts. Cover; let rest for 10 minutes. Roll each part into a 10x6-inch rectangle. Without stretching, fold long side over to within 1 inch of opposite side; seal. Place on greased baking sheets. Cover; let rise till almost double, about 1 hour. Bake at 375° for 15 to 20 minutes or till golden brown. While warm, brush with glaze made of 1 cup sifted confectioners' sugar, 2 tablespoons hot water, and ½ teaspoon butter or margarine. Makes 3 loaves.

Giving is one of the joys of Christmas, but only if the gift be thoughtfully chosen, the receiver flattered by the choice. Here are gift thoughts for some very special people—those to whom a kitchen is a castle and entertaining a glorious adventure. Pick a recipe that's fun to make and fun to eat. Assemble pertinent cooking or serving dishes and all of the canned ingredients. Or present the makings for a yuletide punch combined in a pretty punch bowl to your favorite snack-party hostess. Tuck the recipe inside the gift card. For fun, tuck in a small cutting board and knife. It's perfect—a party-starter for a party-giver.

Give Party-Starters

CHRISTMAS PUNCH

2 quarts cranberry-juice cocktail
Juice of 4 lemons (¾ cup)
1 quart orange juice
½ cup sugar
2 quarts ginger ale, chilled
Thin orange and lemon slices
Halved maraschino cherries

Mix juices and sugar. Pour into punch bowl over ice. Add chilled ginger ale, pouring slowly down side of bowl. Makes about 6 quarts. Trim with floaters: Stack an orange slice, a lemon slice, and a halved cherry. Place on surface of punch.

CHRISTMAS FRUIT BALLS

With the coarse blade of a food grinder, grind together 1½ cups cooked pitted prunes, ½ pound (1½ cups) pitted dates, ¾ cup dried apricots, ½ cup raisins, and 1 cup finely chopped California walnuts. Add ¼ cup sugar and ¼ cup frozen orange juice concentrate, thawed. Form into 1-inch balls; roll in one 3¼-ounce can flaked coconut. Store balls in sealed plastic bag or metal container. Makes about 6 dozen.

More party-starter ideas: For immediate delivery, give an appetizer tray all ready to serve the drop-in guests. Deck a pretty wooden platter with cheese, relishes on toothpicks inserted into a grapefruit, a tiny loaf of bread, crackers, and luncheon meats wrapped in festive colored foil and Christmas ribbon. Add a snowman topper to the relish display and some holly.

OTHER FOOD GIFTS

- *Tea*—Choose a variety of kinds in small containers to send along with a pretty teapot. If you go Oriental, include the tiny Japanese cups.

- *Coffee*—Send a can of espresso or another fancy coffee, an espresso coffee maker, and perhaps a set of tiny cups. Or with regular coffee, include gaily decorated coffee mugs.

- *Preserves, jellies, jams*—If you make your own, nothing's nicer. When you're putting them up, choose interesting jars—all alike if you want to simplify the packaging problem later. And pick pretty go-together colors—red cherry jelly and green mint, orange marmalade, or wine jelly made from an old recipe.

- *A cook book*—plus the ingredients for your favorite recipe therein.

- *Cheese*—Choose a fine cheese and present it under a cheese bell with cheese knife or spreader and a nosegay of holly. Refrigerate.

- *Canned gourmet foods*—Fill a basket with antipasto, fancy soups, stuffed oranges, smoked oysters, and other tidbits that a friend with a taste for the unusual would enjoy.

CHOCOLATE PRETZEL COOKIES

    1 cup sugar
    ½ cup butter or margarine
    2 eggs
    2 1-ounce squares unsweetened
       chocolate, melted
    1 teaspoon vanilla
    2 cups sifted all-purpose flour
    1½ teaspoons baking powder
    ½ teaspoon salt
    ½ teaspoon soda
    ¾ teaspoon cinnamon
    ¼ teaspoon ginger
    ¼ teaspoon allspice

Cream sugar and butter, beating till fluffy. Add eggs, chocolate, and vanilla; beat well. Sift dry ingredients together; stir into creamed mixture; blend well. *Chill thoroughly.*

To form pretzels, roll about 2 teaspoons dough on lightly floured surface to form a 9-inch strip. Place on cookie sheet and twist into pretzel shape. Sprinkle with sugar. Bake at 350° for 10 minutes. Makes about 4 dozen cookies.

MAILING HINTS

To someone away from home, no gift is more appreciated than a box of homemade cookies—provided they arrive whole and still delicious. Be sure that yours will arrive with almost-fresh-from-the-oven goodness.

- *Types*—Choose fairly moist, non-fragile cookies such as fruit-filled drop or bar cookies, brownies, etc. Avoid sticky frostings, and remember that trims such as nuts and chocolate succumb quickly to hot climate.

- *Containers*—Tins and sturdy cardboard boxes are good choices, of course. But pretty coffee cans, plastic sewing boxes, colorful paper gift-wrap sacks, and baskets are all interesting containers for gift cookies and candies.

- *Wrapping*—Use clear plastic wrap, aluminum foil, or waxed paper topped with gift-wrapping paper. Wrap cookies individually, in pairs back-to-back, or in stacks, depending on how fragile they are. Wrap only cookies of the same kind together, so crisp cookies stay crisp and soft cookies stay soft. Bake bar cookies in foil-ware pans; mail in the baking pan.
  Candy like fudge, panocha, and divinity may be poured into a container—a foil pan or a plastic box—then decorated, topped with clear plastic wrap, and sent without cutting. Or, wrap the pieces individually.

- *Packing*—Layer cookies and candies in container one layer at a time. Fill in spaces between with crumbled paper or popcorn. Shake to pack. Separate layers with a piece of cardboard cut to just fit inside container or box.

- *Sending*—Pack containers carefully in sturdy boxes, with plenty of padding. Tie securely and label the packages clearly. Have the post office stamp the packages "Perishable." You may want to send them by air mail, but it's not necessary if you've made a choice of cookies and candies that will keep well.

- *Storage*—You may have to store some cookies while preparing the rest to mail. Keep *crisp* cookies in a loosely covered container in a cool place. Keep soft cookies in an airtight container. If they get hard, add a slice of apple to the container for a few days.
  To freeze baked cookies, pack in freezer containers, stuffing waxed paper or clear plastic wrap between. Thaw at room temperature.

Candies

HONEY SUGARED WALNUTS

Keep a bowl filled with these all during the holidays—

2½ cups California walnut halves
1½ cups sugar
½ cup water
¼ cup honey
½ teaspoon salt
½ teaspoon cinnamon
½ teaspoon vanilla

Toast walnuts in 375° oven 10 minutes, stirring once. Butter sides of heavy 2-quart saucepan. In it combine sugar, water, honey, salt, and cinnamon. Heat and stir till sugar dissolves and mixture boils. Cook to soft-ball stage (236°) without stirring. Remove from heat; beat till mixture begins to get creamy. Add vanilla and warm nuts; stir gently till nuts are well coated and mixture becomes thick. Turn out on buttered baking sheet; with 2 forks, separate nuts at once.

PEANUT POPCORN BALLS

5 cups popped corn
½ cup sugar
½ cup light corn syrup
½ cup crunchy peanut butter
½ teaspoon vanilla

Keep popped corn crispy in 300° oven. Combine sugar and corn syrup in saucepan. Cook stirring constantly, till mixture comes to a full rolling boil. Remove from heat. Stir in peanut butter and vanilla. Immediately pour over warm popcorn; mix gently to coat. With buttered hands, form into 10 popcorn balls.

BUTTERSCOTCH QUICKIES

2 6-ounce packages (2 cups)
    butterscotch pieces
¼ cup peanut butter
5 cups corn flakes

In large saucepan, melt butterscotch pieces and peanut butter over low heat. Remove from heat; add corn flakes and stir till well coated. Drop from teaspoon onto waxed paper. Let stand till firm. Makes about 3½ dozen pieces.

CRYSTAL-CUT CANDIES

2 cups sugar
½ cup light corn syrup
½ cup water
Dash salt
Few drops green food coloring
4 to 6 drops oil of wintergreen

Combine sugar, corn syrup, water, and salt. Bring to boiling. Cook to soft-crack stage (290°). Add coloring and flavoring; gently swirl mixture to blend. Pour into 8x8x2-inch metal pan. Let stand a few minutes till film forms over top. Mark candy in little puffs, each about ¾-inch square. Because candy is cooler at edges, start marking from outside and work toward the center. Using a broad spatula or pancake turner, press a line across pan ¾ inch from edge, *being careful not to break through the film on surface*. Repeat around other 3 sides of pan, intersecting lines at corners to form squares. (If lines do not hold shape, candy is not cool enough.) Continue marking to center.

While waiting for center to cool enough, retrace previous lines, pressing the spatula deeper *but not breaking film*. When spatula may be pressed to bottom of pan in all lines, candy will be shaped in square puffs. Cool, then turn out and break into pieces. Makes 100.

REMARKABLE FUDGE

4 cups sugar
1 14½-ounce can (1⅔ cups) evaporated
    milk
1 cup butter or margarine
1 12-ounce package (2 cups) semisweet
    chocolate pieces
1 pint marshmallow creme
1 teaspoon vanilla
1 cup chopped California walnuts

Butter sides of heavy 3-quart saucepan. In it combine first 3 ingredients. Cook over medium heat to soft-ball stage (236°), stirring frequently. Remove from heat; add chocolate pieces, marshmallow creme, vanilla, and chopped nuts. Beat till chocolate is melted and blended. Pour into buttered 9x9x2-inch pan. Score in squares while warm and top each with a walnut half. Cut when firm. Makes 3 dozen 1½-inch pieces.

Three candies just right for Christmas giving: Baubles of bright green Crystal-cut Candies, failproof Remarkable Fudge with walnut toppers, and puffs of Perfect Divinity.

EASY BUTTER CRUNCH

1 cup butter or margarine
1 cup sugar
1½ cups almond halves
1 6-ounce package (1 cup) semisweet
   chocolate pieces

Melt butter in heavy skillet; stir in sugar. Add almond halves and cook, stirring constantly till mixture is golden brown and almonds begin to pop, about 12 to 14 minutes.

Spread mixture evenly in 15½x10½x1-inch baking pan. Immediately sprinkle with chocolate pieces; spread evenly over candy with knife or small spatula. Cool; when chocolate is set, crack candy into pieces. Store in metal container. Can be frozen several weeks. Makes 1 pound.

PERFECT DIVINITY

2½ cups sugar
½ cup light corn syrup
½ cup water
   • • •
2 egg whites
1 teaspoon vanilla
½ cup chopped candied cherries

In a heavy 2-quart saucepan, combine sugar, corn syrup, and water. Cook to soft-ball stage (236°), stirring only till sugar dissolves. Meanwhile, beat egg whites till stiff peaks form. When syrup reaches 236°, gradually add *half* the syrup to egg whites beating at high speed on electric mixer. Cook remaining syrup to hard-ball stage (250°). Slowly add to the egg white mixture, beating constantly.

Add vanilla and beat till candy holds its shape (about 5 minutes). If desired, add chopped candied cherries. Drop pillows of candy from a teaspoon onto waxed paper, swirling tops. Makes about 3 dozen pieces of candy.

WALL DECORATIONS

Walls, too, should sparkle with holiday brilliance and they can at the cost of very little time and effort. The secret is to see what you and your imagination can do with the materials you have on hand. If you are a start-from-scratch creator, you'll originate many ideas.

Walls come to the assistance of the suppressed designer when there isn't any more floor or table space available. Small apartments may be unable to give up space even to one branching evergreen. Vertical, horizontal, and circular hanging symbols may be placed between windows, on dividing partitions, and on sliding window walls. By creating in scale to the space available and by adapting colors that are harmonious to the established color scheme, the room will stand as festive as any other. Candles and spotlights assist by picking up highlights and pinpointing handiwork to best advantage for near or not-so-near viewing.

So many materials can be adapted to wall symbols. Evergreens and Christmas balls can be taped to the wall or to a backing and then hung. A needle and thread can turn out exquisite stitchery designs. And paper and glue will always be versatile favorites for creating.

Biretta-like wall plaques are fashioned of equilateral triangles of construction paper. Each triangle has one side sprayed gold, the other left the original hue. Triangle points overlap and four units staple together. Then gold foil trims decorate edges and points.

Felt hanging is made from assorted geometric cutouts. Glue holds the shapes to the background. Attach a rod to the top and hang. Try original designs or copy a favorite Christmas card.

An antique Italian liturgical candlestick, topped by a flaming, short, red candle, flanks one side of the attractive and fanciful arrangement at the left. An illuminated Gregorian chant on parchment rests on the right. The wall grouping consists of long-needle pine boughs wired to a long strip of chicken wire which is taped and tacked to the wall.

Nestled among the boughs are a toy violin, snare drum, mandolin, cornet, and bugle. The warmth of the woods of the violin and mandolin are echoed in the wood of the French Empire chest, and in the browns of the wall.

Hat racks, expandable ones purchased at a dime store for about 18 cents, form the base for the handsome wall decoration at the right, the racks are sprayed yellow, then wrapped with metallic gold and red velvet ribbon strands. Ribbon attaches to the racks with white liquid cement. Glass tree baubles suspended in the middle of each diamond shape, provide a pleasing sparkle for the ornament which may be dismantled to free the rack after Christmas.

Spools form the outlines for this fanciful tree designed to enhance a colorful slab-style door or plain wall. Brilliant yarns fill in the design of the tree assembled on perforated hardboard backing. Cut spools in half and glue around the border and into the shape of a tree. Use a whole spool at each corner. Weave yarn around the spools and top each with gummed seals. Use brilliant yarn colors that will be visible from a distance.

Eight-point stars, simple but very effective, decorate this space above a fireplace.

Cut eight-point stars from 22-inch cardboard squares. Make four long points to corners of square, four short points to centers of sides. Cut similar star from a 16-inch square in another color. Cut a four-pointed, star-shaped hole from the center of the smaller stars. Trim edges with gold tape and seals. Glue four spools to back of small stars near points of center hole. Glue four spools to large star and join stars.

Felt flower wall tree, pictured below, can be made as a group project of the entire family. Let Father build the background for the tree. Then have one person cover the panels while the rest of the family cut and create felt flowers. Mother can pin the flowers in place once the panels are covered.

To copy the design, cut a 22x31-inch panel of composition board or heavy corrugated cardboard. Soft wood may also be used, but the cardboard or composition boards are more manageable for cutting and for pinning into. Cover the panel with burlap, pulling the fabric to the back side and taping to hold. Attach the panel to a slightly larger panel bordered with felt and mitered at the corners. Attach a wire or string to the back for hanging.

Cut multicolored swatches of felt into circles ranging from one inch to three inches in size. Snip into circles to form points or petals to get a variety of shapes. Center some of the flowers with plain circles for contrast. Pin flowers to the background at different heights using hatpins. Flowers may be juggled until a satisfactory design is achieved, in this case, a seasonal Christmas tree. After Christmas, the felt flowers may be removed to convert the panel into an attractive family bulletin board.

Tissue tube wall tree will make a popular classroom project. Start youngsters saving tissue tubes several weeks before Christmas.

To reproduce the design, cover a 24x48-inch piece of hardboard or heavy cardboard with gold wall- or gift paper. Cover half of a 30-inch plastic foam cone with red fabric or paper. Glue cone to the background. Wrap nine tissue rolls with pink tissue paper, seven tubes with orange tissue paper, and four tubes with turquoise tissue paper. Trim each tube with ribbon or cloth as in the picture. Glue the cones to each other side by side.

Glue the cones in tiers. Cover one tube with shocking pink paper, trim and glue it to the top of the tree. Finish with a gold foil star. Wrap a 4x7-inch shallow box with paper to resemble a tree base and glue it to the background. Trim it, also, with sewing notions or ribbon before mounting on background. Add a wire to back for hanging.

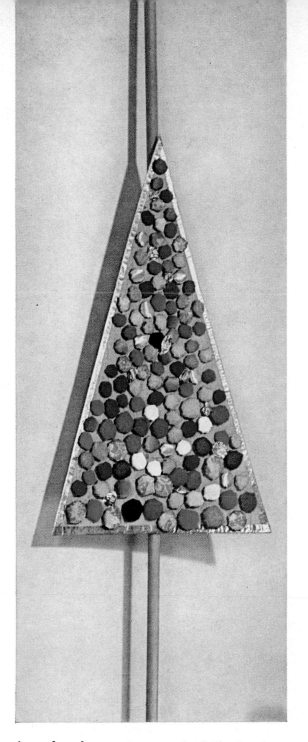

Blue and green fringe ball tree smartly matches the colors of the flowered chair and rug, and the blue of the wall in this room. The tree size and style also complement the Spanish-flavored decor of the entire room.

To reproduce the tree, wrap yarn 50 times around a three-inch-wide piece of cardboard. Slide the loops off the cardboard, tie them in the center, and cut the ends of the yarn. Fluff to form into mushroom shapes. Pin or glue the tufts to a plastic foam half-cone. Add a wicker basket base and a glitter and tissue circle for the top and attach the entire design to the wall.

A push pole can give great flexibility in where you place your Christmas wall decorations as this triangle puff tree illustrates. The tree begins with a 2x3½-foot triangle of cardboard covered with Japanese gold splattered paper adhered with rubber cement. Next, upholstery fabric was cut into a triangle slightly smaller than the cardboard triangle and into four-inch circles. The outer edges of the circles were loosely basted, then pulled together. Cotton batting was stuffed inside the circles and they were sewed to the fabric triangle. Finally, the triangle was glued to foil, stitched, and wired to unused pushpole.

Stylized wall tree below stands 39 inches high. Eight-inch triangles of construction paper sprayed gold on one side are creased into four 4-inch triangles with the gold side up (see diagram below). The points are stapled together with a ¾ inch overlap. After units are stapled together in pyramid-like fashion, they are glued to a cardboard backing about ½ inch smaller than outside edge of finished decoration. Paper stars finish design.

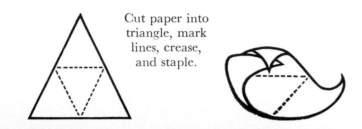

Cut paper into triangle, mark lines, crease, and staple.

The Partridge in a Pear Tree inspired this stunning holiday wall panel. Easily reproduced, the panel has a linen background topped by felt pieces cut into the tree shape, leaf shapes in different sizes and colors, pears, and the partridge. White liquid cement adheres the felt to the background.

A long wooden dowel stained dark to match the other room furnishings slips through a hem stitched into the top of the hanging. Small weights on the bottom keep the hanging smooth.

A colorful accent for any room in the house, the wall tree at the right is made of crepe-paper flowers. The blue and green flowers have three layers of crepe-paper strips machine-stitched on one edge (or hand stitched), leaving end threads long and unfastened. The other edge is fringed by cutting strips about three fourths of the way across width of strips. Finally, the stitch threads are drawn up to gather the crepe paper. This gathered strip then encircles the edge of a half plastic foam ball covered with crepe paper. Additional folded and ruffled blue-crepe paper wraps around the plastic foam balls in several narrow layers before green is added.

The flowers vary in diameter from three to eight inches. They are attached with tape and wire to a central round curtain rod support that is inserted in a painted wood block base resting on the floor. The four flowers extending out from the central shaft have heavy wire branches. Chenille-covered wire outlines the tree shaft and branches. The rod support allows the tree to be mobile and free of wall attachments.

Crepe paper wall tree and garland team to make use of every inch of seven pieces of crepe paper lengths measuring 14x36 inches. This is accomplished by machine-stitching the seven pieces together down the center length and trimming to a triangular tree shape with trunk. Tree shape has triangles cut out of each side to leave triangle branches cut nearly to stitch line.

Gold braid covers the stitching to achieve a finished appearance. A gold metallic embossed star tops tree. The cutout triangles stitched onto a long ribbon and topped by braid, gold seals, and stars create a garland effect above the tree. Additional gold ribbon, two strips, swings above the garland and drops along the sides for extended length. Gold seals attach to the wall haphazardly around crepe-paper tree and garland.

148

Wall wreath hanging speaks its piece in traditional Christmas color language. Materials needed to duplicate it include: one yard white felt; $2\frac{1}{8}$ yards $\frac{1}{2}$-inch metallic gold braid; $4\frac{1}{2}$ yards two-inch width hunter green satin blanket binding; 17 red Christmas ornaments; 5/7 yard $1\frac{1}{2}$-inch width red satin ribbon; 15-inch dowel $\frac{1}{4}$ inch in diameter; gold paint; white glue.

To make the hanging, paint the dowel gold and let it dry. Now, cut the felt to 15x 17-inch size; glue gold braid around the outside edges of the felt; miter the corners. Cut two five-inch gold braid pieces, fold them horizontally to form loops. Glue the loops to the wrong side, $2\frac{1}{2}$ inches in from the edges on one narrow end of the hanging. Next, cut green blanket binding into three equal lengths. Braid the strips loosely to a two-inch width. In scattered groups, hand-tack the red ball ornaments onto the braided strip. Shape the strip into a circle, glue it on felt with the ends at the upper right side of felt. Using $\frac{5}{8}$-inch red ribbon, tie a bow, glue it in place to conceal the ends of the wreath. Insert the dowel through the braid loops, glue to avoid slipping.

Wall hangings in bright hues will give your home a festive appearance. To make any of the three on the right, hem the top edge of 8x40-inch piece of felt to form dowel casing. Divide panel into quarters and outline with gold braid, rickrack, or soutache. Mark letters in center of each square, outline with glue, and press trim into the glue.

Insert a nine-inch gold painted dowel through the casing at the top. Use metallic soutache braid for hanging string, tying at both ends of dowel.

Abstract banners at the left, both boldly colored, could herald in the Christmas season. Both designs, stitched primarily by machine, have contrasting threads highlighting the outlines. Zigzag and other fancy stitches add further interest. Burlap or felt can be used for the background. Since felt stretches, the cutout pieces are glued in place to secure them to the felt background before they are machine-stitched. Hang banners with a dowel and braid.

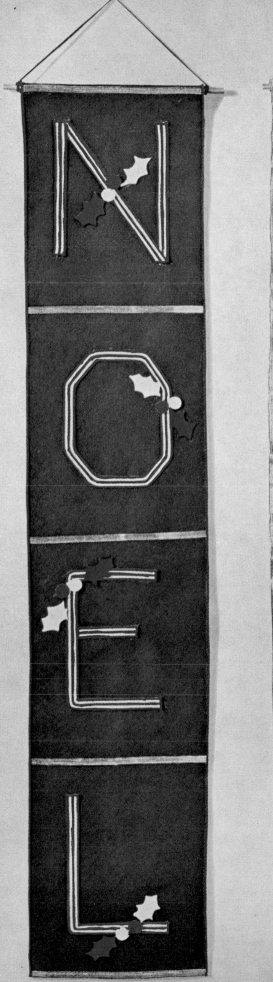
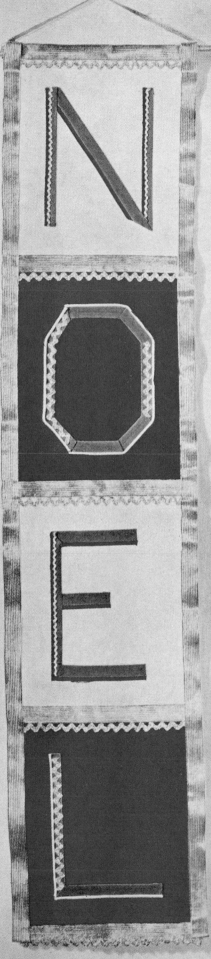

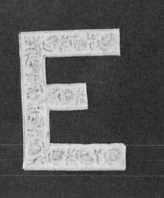

Partridge wall hanging has deep blue felt background measuring 13½x18 inches. Partridges use scraps of turquoise and chartreuse felt; they perch on branches made of metallic gold soutache braid. Two and a half yards metallic gold fringe form border for hanging. Metallic gold baby rickrack gives details to birds, two sequins become eyes. All trims are glued with white liquid cement as is casing made by folding felt at top to hold dowel hanger.

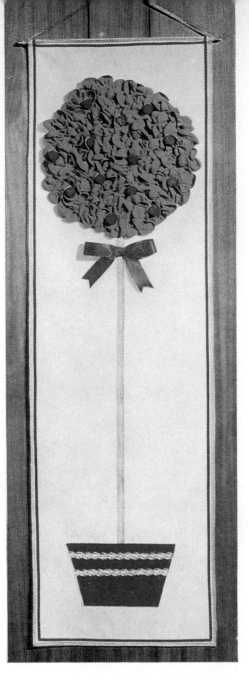

Three Kings wall banners have felt exterior backed by suede cloth. Felt figures, cut in tapered rectangle attached to back by hand-stitching, have sequin trim. Faces and crowns are made of small felt scraps cut to correct shapes. Gold braid outlines each of the banners and yarn tassels, in colors that match the Kings, finish the trim. Banners are hung from cut-down curtain rods.

Topiary tree has 12x40-inch background of white felt, 12-inch diameter circle top of green felt. Giant rickrack is shirred tightly by sewing down the center and pulling the thread. Glue the gathered rickrack to the felt circle and trim with ball fringe. Next, cut a red felt base with 7¼-inch top, five-inch bottom. Add braid.

Glue on a gold braid trunk topped with a red satin bow. Add the base. Trim outside of edges of hanging.

This eye-pleasing wall decoration can easily be made in about an hour once you've gathered the necessary materials. It is versatile and can hang anywhere or a smaller version could embellish the top of a gift box.

To reproduce the design, enlarge the pattern below and place it on a piece of yellow-green felt which is folded in half. The felt should measure 26x32 when folded widthwise. Cut out the sections as indicated by the solid lines on the pattern to achieve the openwork tree.

Now, using the pattern again, cut the jardiniere from a small piece of bright red felt. Glue the pot to the center area of the felt panel at the spot indicated.

Glue large, round, gold spangles as decorations on the jardiniere. Center each spangle with a bead. Glue red, blue, green, and gold sequins and stars to the tree at one-inch intervals. Top the tree with shiny star sequins arranged in an inverted T-shape. Center each with a bead.

Fold the felt panel under one inch at the top and bottom. Glue folds in place to form slots for holding metal rods or wood dowels. Spray-paint two wood drawer knobs and attach them to the rod ends. Tie metallic gold cording to each end of the dowel at top to hang.

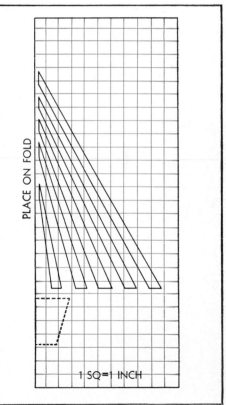

PLACE ON FOLD

1 SQ=1 INCH

The long ristras of chili peppers drying in the sun in the Southwest suggested to a New Mexican the idea of making a wreath from which to cut the pods as needed to be ground for regional recipes. To make the wreath, spray paint a plastic foam wreath red. Wire fresh "Chili Colorado" peppers to the ring individually. Place the wreath in the sun to dry the peppers. At the top add a lavish green velvet bow and a pair of scissors suspended with a narrow green velvet ribbon. Clip off the dried pepper pods as they are needed.

Try similar wreaths with other material used or made in the kitchen. Wrap home-made candies in cellophane and wire them to the wreath, or wrap dried fruit (dates, figs, and others) in cellophane and snip them off for snacks. Colorful gourds can also be attached to a wreath for a regional wall design.

Wood clothespins form this novelty wreath, a variation of the wreath on page 159. To copy the design, cut 17½-inch wreath from ¼-inch thick plywood. Make band 1¼ inches wide. Finish wreath with interior-exterior wood stain, adhere a ring of felt to back to protect wall surface.

Sand clothespins, dip in stain, allow to set, following directions on container. Glue clothespins to frame, alternating as in pattern. At inner circumference pins will touch; at outer circumference pins will flare out slightly. Spray pins with clear plastic before gluing in place. Form center wreath by stacking and gluing nuts and pods to pins. Spray entire wreath with two coats of clear plastic.

Softly rolled magnolia leaves that have been sprayed with a metallic gold spray paint "grow" around a wire base to create this festive wreath. Copy wreath for a protected outside door, for over your fireplace, or for a stair railing.

Begin wreath by coiling several lengths of light-weight wire. Twist ends together to secure in shape of a wreath. Spray-paint artificial magnolia leaves with wired stems, or glycerin-treat live leaves before spraying with metallic gold paint. Wire leaves in position. Top with a giant velvet bow.

Antique scale and coffee grinder have been related to colorful felt flower wreath, rather than moving them from the kitchen for Christmas decorating.

The designer started with a 12-inch plastic foam wreath doughnut cut flat on the back side as a foundation. She concealed the base with strips of complementary green crepe paper glued to the plastic foam.

After covering the wreath she wired it to a green-painted rattan mat. Then gay felt flowers were cut into circles measuring from one to three inches in diameter. Edges were snipped and flowers were pinned to wreath.

Plant labelers, made of wood and available at any nursery or garden supply store, are used to shape these smart wall decorations. Paint the stakes in the desired colors and glue them, when thoroughly dry, to a flat plywood or heavy cardboard disk. The heights of the garden labels above measure 24½, 12½, and 8½ inches. Make smaller ones to blend with the large star.

Muffin cups and paper honeycomb balls make a two-way wreath that is finished on both sides to hang on a glass door or window if desired. Plastic foam wreath is 12 inches in diameter and uses 48 small cake cups, 68 paper balls, 68 pearl-headed corsage pins, 68 sequins, all pinned in place around the wreath.

Multicolor-wreath from luncheon and cocktail-size napkins makes an inexpensive decoration. Fold napkins into cornucopias by overlapping edges and stapling. Staple napkins over 6, 9, 12-inch wire rings. Conceal staples with seals. Hang rings concentrically.

This snowball star's angular lines repeat the lines of the shiny brass frame of the bed standing below it.

The star starts with a 22-inch in diameter colored cardboard circle edged with 18 triangular notches that measure two inches across and three inches deep. White and metallic gold blended yarn laces through each notch and around every arm from side to side and diagonally to form a star shape.

A five-inch in diameter, store-bought, paper sphere glues in the center of the star. Two rows of identical, but smaller, blue and green paper balls held by hatpins encircle the white central ball. A second length of white and gold yarn laces around balls, across star, and through notches to divide star points.

Back of the star has a plastic foam ring attached to keep the hatpins from marring walls. Spools or plastic foam balls might be attached instead to provide protection.

Foil reflector wreath begins with an 18-inch diameter, beveled plastic foam wreath wrapped with strips of red crepe paper. Then disassembled layers of store-bought foil flowers top foil reflectors, usually used behind tree lights, arrange around wreath. Florist pins secure flowers by lacing through large glass-bead ornaments, flower layers, reflectors to pierce plastic foam wreath.

Painted wood candlesticks in front of wreath hold gold glass finials with florist clay concealed by matching foil reflectors.

For crisp wreath at right, you will need eight-inch-square doilies and a 15-inch wire ring. Form the doilies into cornucopia, overlapping to fit the pattern of lace; staple in place.

Fold the point of each cornucopia over the wire ring, with point of doily on back of cornucopia; staple close to the wire ring.

Staple the cornucopias together, side by side, near the outer edges. Decorate the wreath inside the top with a large green ribbon bow.

Cornucopia wreaths can be made from stiff paper or stiffened fabric, as well as from the doilies, for wreaths just as attractive.

Placemat straw wall grouping begins with 12-inch in diameter cardboard circle. Covered with brilliantly hued tissue paper, it glues to a 12-inch in diameter plastic foam wreath. An eight-inch diameter circle of contrasting color paper glues to the 12-inch circle. Next, a six-inch diameter cardboard circle covered with paper glues to empty thread spool, adheres to the 12-inch circle. Two more tissue paper circles with a 4- and 3½-inch diameter adhere to center of the six-inch diameter circle.

Sticks from reed placemats are sprayed gold, covered by large glitter flakes. They insert into the plastic foam wreath to complete the design.

Wheat wreath duo begins with 2x7½-inch length of corrugated cardboard cut to keep the grooves vertical to 2-inch measurement. Paper facing one side of the cardboard is peeled off to expose grooves. One wheat stalk is placed in each groove, except for about ¾ inch from each end of rectangle. Strip of masking tape adheres across to secure wheat. Duplicate assembly is made, two are stacked, and the end flaps are taped together. Front of cardboard is covered with 2¾-inch-wide velvet ribbon. Flap ends insert in front opening of round stovepipe chimney collar, bowing cardboard. Assembly flaps are taped with adhesive to back of collar. Row of gold legal seals adds finished touch. Wire hanger tapes to the back. Entire procedure is repeated to duplicate the second wreath.

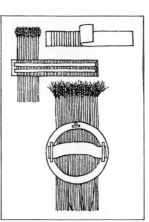

Red satin-finish bow tops inventive clothespin wreath. New clothespins are glued to narrow, heavyweight cardboard ring. Pins are alternated, head in and head out for texture. Once positioned, they are shellacked for a shiny effect. Next, selected marzipan fruit is wired to cardboard backing with fine wire. Marzipan is confection of ground almonds, sugar, egg white, combined to make paste, shaped to form fruit, then dried. The green leaves are artificial ones which can be purchased at a variety store. For ease in handling, wire all fruit together first onto one long medium-weight wire.

The traditional wreath will always be a favorite Christmas wall embellishment. This wreath, hanging in an entrance hall, is made from lacy pine sprigs wired to a plastic foam base. Plastic foam is first spray-painted green, then clusters of greens are wired to it. Frosted artificial miniature fruit wires to the evergreen sprigs for a Della Robbia effect.

Repeating the texture and colors, additional pine sprigs and candied fruit combine with Christmas packages dressed in the same greens and gold on the buffet top below the wreath.

Sixteen-ray star of lightweight cardboard and bright-hued yarn is color coordinated with a prized antique desk and chair and hung on a wall nearby the two. The star begins with 16 pieces of 6x12-inch size colored cardboard. Each piece is divided lengthwise into four equal parts, scored along these lines, bent, and overlapped one quarter. Staples or glue hold the cardboard in prism shapes measuring 1½ inches on each side by 12 inches in length. Next, cotton rug yarn winds around these 16 rays, allowing spaces of cardboard to show through between the strands of heavy yarn for special color and texture effect.

The sixteen arms are then laid in the form of a star on a 22-inch in diameter circle, leaving a six-inch in diameter space in the center. After being traced onto the cardboard circle, a parallel star is cut out. The yarn covered prisms slip over each new ray and are taped along the back to hold. A felt-covered plastic foam disk edged in burlap fringe fills the center of the starburst. The burlap centerpiece is topped by a cardboard doughnut wrapped in yarn to match the outer fringed area that is neatly pinned and glued to secure in place.

This stylized wreath has the wire base of a discarded lampshade for its framework. Cotton tape, generally used in cloth-covered shades, wraps around the wire. Four spools attach to the frame back to add design depth.

Teardrop art paper petals measuring 3½ inches at the widest part and six inches long glue to the frame. Paper circles decorated with glitter, leaves, snowflakes, sunbursts, and other designs (no two alike) fasten to the rounded end of the teardrops. Packages continue color scheme.

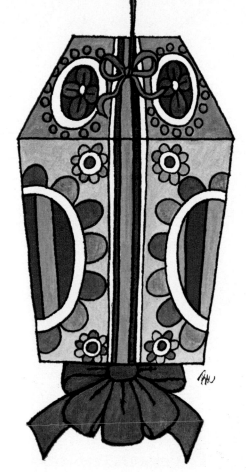

GIFT WRAPS AND CARDS

Festively wrapped holiday packages help make modest gifts appear more elegant and extravagant presents seem even more lavish. It's all in choosing the right wrap for the right gift.

This year, spend some time to plan gift wrappings that will complement the receivers of your presents. For those special recipients, list the interests, background, and personality to get ideas for an original wrap. The possibilities are as abundant as the personality variances among your friends.

Wrapping materials are abundant. Besides the traditional gift papers, use materials, sewing trims, sacks, Christmas card cutouts, and imagination!

There is something extra special about receiving a handcrafted Christmas card. And there is always extra pride in sending one. You don't need to be a professional artist to create clever designs, all you need are a few tools and some time. For a handsome look, try silk-screening the design. Or create cards from cutout paper. Ideas are everywhere!

Hair clips and curls of yarn hair top demure face of package wrap design below. Eyelashes and lips cut from construction paper are glued to adhesive-back paper face, beads are glued to neck. Cotton lace attached with glue to box at right forms face with straw hair. Gumdrops are eyes.

Silver-blue box with six sides below was covered with velvet and lamé. Fold heavy cardboard rectangle into six divisions. Cut elongated ovals along lines. Tape sides together. Trace around top and bottom onto cardboard; cut out bottom piece; glue in place. Cover box with velvet. Make smaller container for inside, but do not cut top piece. Drape with silver lamé cloth; line with aluminum foil. Insert container inside larger one, glue to base. Cover box top with velvet; glue glass ball in position; tape to box.

Spire-like box was designed using construction board for sides and top. Box was covered with blue velvet. Peaked lid was formed of construction board cut to shape, covered with velvet. Silver braid trims edges, silver medallion decorates one side.

Triangular box covered with magenta and blue tissue paper was ready-made. Box and lid were covered separately. Tissue was coated with clear shellac. Triangular pieces of paper were glued to lid, then center was filled with glitter on wet glue. Matching strip of paper banded edge.

Lantern box is outside construction board hexagon and inside smaller hexagon. Lid for outside box was made with six triangular sides, lined with tissue, topped with glass ball. Theatrical gelatin rectangles were cut to fit section of sides, glued on inside to show through openings cut in sides. Inside box lifts out with ribbon loop attached to sides.

Simple magenta box was covered with tissue paper; braid and velvet ribbon were glued around the lid.

Paper bags in many colors shape humorous Christmas figures. One bag is placed under the other to seal both ends. The faces are contrasting paper glued to the bags with features applied with poster paint. The feet are glued to the bottom of the base bag. The hands are cut from brown construction paper or from brown paper bags. Other lines for legs and feet are also drawn on with paint. People bags are perfect for bottle gifts.

Try using fruit designs when you have to wrap a gift on short notice. They are easy to do and very effective. Or, if you prefer, use vegetable cutouts.

To copy these, you need only gift paper, a variety of paper scraps, India ink, and glue. Most any kind and color paper will work for the fruit designs.

Begin with simplified outlines of fruit, then work up to stylized versions of your own. For variety, use shelf or wallpaper with fruits in the design; then enlarge one of the fruits for the cutout pattern. After fruit is glued in place, use pen and ink to add the accent lines and markings.

Elegant packages on the left are beribboned, bejewelled, and bestriped. Wrapping materials include satin, taffeta, ribbon, and rickrack. Beribboned box has a cover made like a slip-cover with one end left open. The other end is secured with a snap fastener. Three strips of velvet ribbon wrap widest sides of the box.

The bejewelled and bestriped boxes have separately wrapped tops and bases. Gold trim outlines fabric cutout on gold box and black ribbon trim glues to the lid and base of the orange box. Ball fringe is glued around the lid bottom.

Ice cream cartons covered with foil and standard wrapping paper form the Near-Eastern city gift boxes above. The doors were cut from old Christmas cards and glued to the cartons. Fold-out bells, available commercially from variety and gift stores, top the cartons. To these tops are added tree balls. Gold foil paper outlines the tops and bottoms, decorating two cartons.

To create a city, display the gift boxes on a table and place them on colorfully wrapped rectangular or square boxes. Select boxes for variety in size and style for pleasing design.

Red enameled box with yarn design, above, will be child's play for you to make, if "Skin the Cat" was one of your favorite childhood games. The box and lid were wrapped separately with red glossy paper. Corrugated cardboard was glued to the inside of the lid and florist pins were pushed into the lid at spaced intervals. Center pin was threaded with several beads. Gold-colored string was woven around the pins forming overlapping squares and octagons. On the sides of lower part of box, pins were pierced through top and bottom rims and through the center of sides to form diamond shapes.

Sewing basket box, above, can be a commercial box with a colorful lid, or a box with the lid covered with glossy paper. Lid and base should be wrapped separately. Wool yarn was threaded on a needle and wrapped around edge of rim, lacing at each corner to the inside; going up one time and down the next time, so that it was not only secure, but neat inside. Glue added to inside corner of lacing secured yarn. Then lengths of rickrack and binding tape were glued around upright sides of box and centered with wool yarn. The same technique was repeated on the lower part of the box.

Red and purple interlaced box, effective but simply executed, was covered with glossy pa-

per. Velvet ribbons were glued to inside rim of lid beginning at a corner and working diagonally, and weaving ribbons along the way. Tissue paper was glued inside lid to conceal ends of ribbons. Small gold ornaments wired at cross points of ribbon added texture.

Decorator box began with the lid being wrapped with midnight blue paper. Next, various size squares and rectangles were cut from green and blue papers, contrasting snowflakes were glued with the squares and rectangles to the box lid. When glue dried, box was given a coat of shellac to give the paper depth.

Cherry box in red and green was covered with red glossy paper, then shiny green ribbon strips were glued to the inside of the lid rim and the inside of the rim of the box bottom. This allowed the box to be opened and closed without damaging it. Ribbons on the lid were aligned with those on the bottom of the box. On the lid only, red string was woven with the green to outline the ribbon. White-headed florist pins were positioned on either side of the ribbon at the lower edge of the rim, string was tied around the pins, working first on one side, then on the other side. The interior of the lid and box bottom were lined with colorful tissue to conceal the ribbon ends.

Christmas lantern box, below, was constructed of illustration board, covered with gold paper, and lined with blue and black paper. Seams of top piece, which was cut from disassembled lid of box, were concealed by glued-on blue ribbon running from corner rims to bow at peak.

Panel designs for box were cut from blue-toned paper, as were tree motifs on box lid. Gift card was made of matching gold paper and decorated with tree motif to match box lid.

Lattice-worked box in red and gold began with a giant gift box from a department store. Picture window openings were cut from each side of box, leaving only frames. Then lattice-work designs were sketched and cut out on light posterboard and taped on inside of the box. Finally, squares of Christmas red velour paper was used to line the inside of the box.

Candlelight box on wall, below, was designed by interlocking a shoe box and shallow halves of square boxes. Inside and outside of boxes were covered with red, blue, and gold paper, the top of box was decorated with bits and scraps of contrasting blue and red paper and felt.

Christmas-tree box top was wrapped separately from bottom, topped with a felt tree shape. Tree was decorated with yarn flowers centered by felt, felt flowers centered with more felt.

Three-dimensional flower boxes had box tops covered with paper with corrugated cardboard glued to the inside. Flowers cut in various colors of paper were pierced with long pins, glued to hold; then pins were pushed into box top. Inside of box and lid were then lined with paper. Finally, a clear spray coating was applied to give the boxes an enameled appearance.

Happy faced packages are covered with wrapping paper. Angel has foam ball head; yarn hair; cork nose. Gift seals form collar, cuffs. Girl holding fan is of construction paper; fan is wallpaper. Boy's hat is newspaper cutout.

Cheery Christmas package-wrap ideas are 12-inch-square boxes with red and white striped paper wrappings encircled by one-inch-wide ribbon.

Figures are cut out of one-inch-thick plastic foam sheets. The boxes may be fastened to the bodies and the hands attached separately, or heads, feet, and hands may be cut separately and attached to the boxes. Either glue or toothpicks may be used as an adherent.

Hatband of snowman is red velour paper; hat is sprayed black. Santa has velour hat. Features are paper.

Containers for cookies: at left, cook's hat is made from paper napkin glued on a coffee can, with paper face and nose; drum is fashioned with two paper plates, punched out holes for ribbons and paper for body. Egg carton is covered with felt and trimmed.

Ordinary shopping bags from your local grocery store can help you create Christmas package wrappings that can't be found ready-made. Or you can start with colored bags. To color your own, use spray paint. Trim with a design which is proportioned for the gift shape.

Props to use are felt, colored construction paper, gummed reinforcements, satin-finished ribbon, sequins, or gumdrops. Other items might include favorite cartoons and cutouts from comic books, sewing trims, and Christmas tree ornaments. If bags are wrinkled, press with a steam iron using added pressure.

Santa Claus face bag has top finished by folding over mouth opening, pasting to secure. Tree bag ties together at top with ribbon.

Silk screening is a form of stenciling a design on paper or fabric. It involves a simple process in which a covering design or background is fastened to a fabric screen. Pattern is printed by pulling silk screen process paint across stencil with a squeegee. There are many variations of the method. The following directions describe a practical way for a beginner to excel.

First decide upon a simple design with a brilliant color scheme. Use a sharp stencil knife or single-edged razor blade to cut the stencil. Almost any kind of thin, nonabsorbent paper such as tracing or typewriter bond paper, will work very well. For each color used, a new sheet of paper will be needed. Place register marks on sides of paper to help line up the design.

Next, prepare the printing frame which is hinged to a flat smooth board as shown in 4 on page 173 (also available commercially). Tack nylon organdy tightly and evenly to one side of the frame. Stretch the screen to the opposite side of the frame in the center. Attach, working from center to corners. Repeat on other two sides vertical to you to be sure to get an even and drumlike fit. Cover the tacks with masking tape. Brush clear liquid shellac over the tape so it will last throughout all cleanings.

Tape stencils face down on printing frame with ¾-inch masking tape as in 2. This will seal frame to prevent leaks in printing process. Use household plastic cement for adhering trouble-

Bearded cats and smiling witches, creatures of all kinds take wondrous new shapes in the imaginations of children. The charm of drawings made by children was captured in these delightful silk screened cards above and at the left.

Inspiration for greeting cards can come from anywhere. As illustrated, children's drawings make clever card ideas. Other possibilities are last year's Christmas cards, calendars, paintings, children's books, and your own imagination. Be sure that the lines are simple and the colors vibrant for the most effective cards.

some areas of stencil. Flip frame down, tape bottom sides as in 3 to avoid leakage when printing. If designs are small, tape several on one screen leaving an inch or more between, covering areas not being used with wax paper on underside. Mend weak areas with clear fingernail polish.

For a squeegee use very hard cardboard such as the backing of art paper pads, rubber tile, or regular commercial type. Cardboard offers the greatest size variety and is disposable. The important thing is, however, that the scraping edge is stiff and even.

Begin printing, working from light to dark colors. Transparent base paint added to colors will make them more transparent. Paint should barely pour for best results. Try several practice runs before beginning. Pour some paint into one of the printing frames held at an angle as in 4 to avoid running. Place frame in printing position as in 5, draw squeegee across inside with firm, even pressure. Then drag paint across frame in same manner to make a print. Lift frame, remove card to dry as in 6.

Follow these step-by-step directions to achieve professional-looking cards you can silk screen yourself. One-by-twos make the simple frame to be used again and again.

Another child's drawing that inspired a silk screened card is this charming Scottish jump-roper.

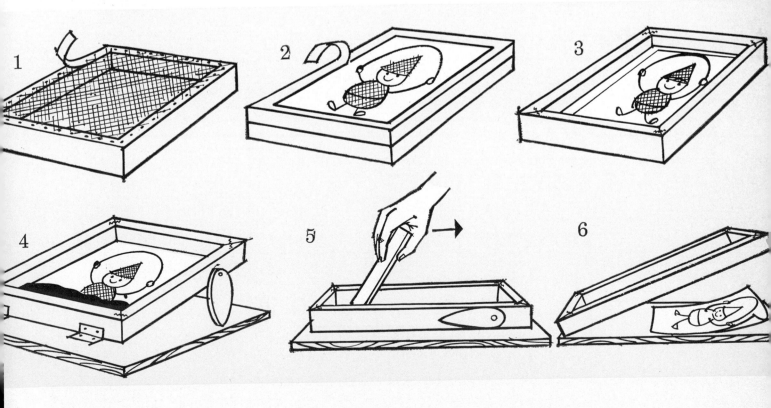

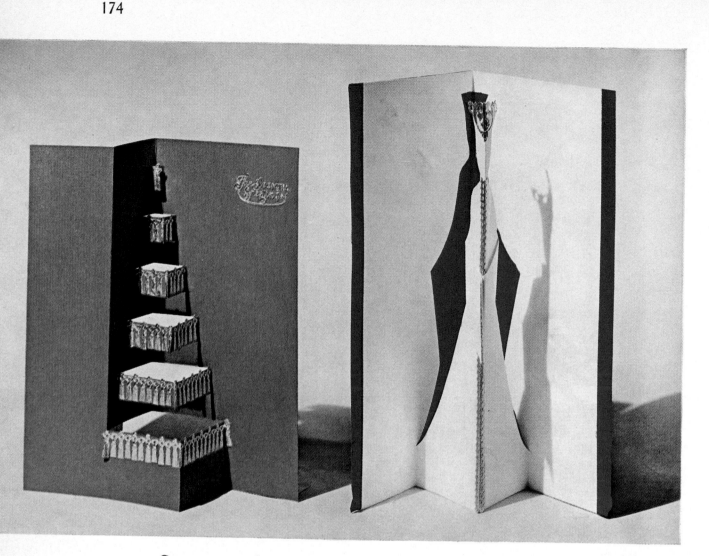

Green tree card: fold a square piece of paper in half, then fold one half in half the opposite direction. In pairs, cut horizontal slits on solid lines, fold on lines where the illustration indicates.

Wise Man: cut figure on solid lines using pattern on right. Fold on dotted lines.

Green construction paper will serve as workable material for making the Christmas card which simulates the symbolic evergreen tree. With only two folds, eleven clips with your scissors, and some embossed gold paper tassels, you can make cards quickly and in quantity. A gold embossed greeting glues to the upper right corner. Greeting could be Christmas card cutout.

Red construction paper with an overlay of white paper created contrasting third dimension for Christmas card with a stylized figure of a wise man garbed in a robe edged with gold trim. Connect the hands of the king by gluing the embossed gold trim over them. Cut the king out of the lightweight white paper only. Glue the white paper to a solid piece of red paper. Follow the patterns and directions for cutting the king and tree at the left.

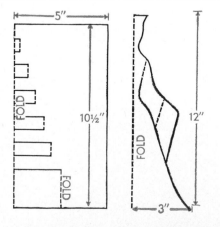

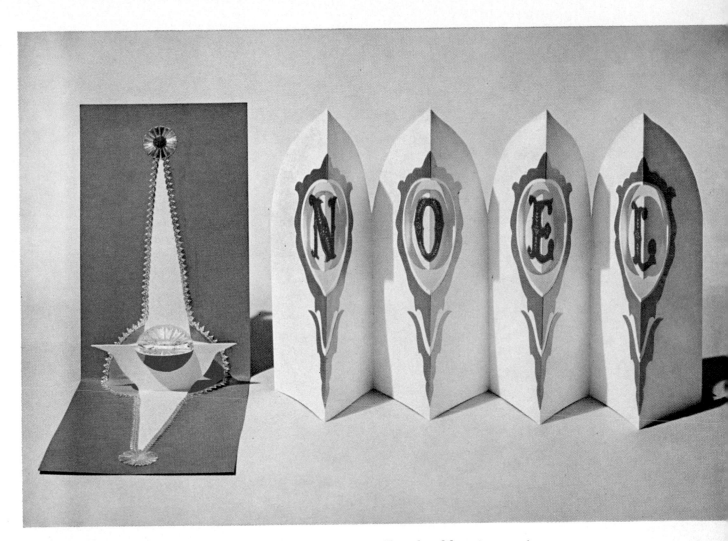

Three different colors of construction paper are used to copy this bright card which boasts a pop-up version of a gay Christmas tree ball. Begin with a basic green piece of paper, top with a pink circle of lighter weight paper, and complete with a yellow shape cut from the pattern at the right. Edge with gold foil paper trimming and top points of the yellow spires with gold seals for a smart finish.

Seven folds of white construction paper and only five cuts with your scissors will shape this seasonal Noel greeting card. Fashion letters of your own, or use the plastic transfer letters which come in all sizes and styles. Use gold wrapping paper for trim. To cut out the card, follow the pattern and directions provided at the right.

Another type of card to make is a gift tag or thank you note. Make it to match the greeting card using the same pattern but scaling it to a smaller size.

For bauble above, glue pink circle on green rectangle, center yellow shape cut from pattern below. Finish with gold trim.

For Noel card, fold long piece of paper eight times in equal widths. Cut on solid lines; fold on dotted.

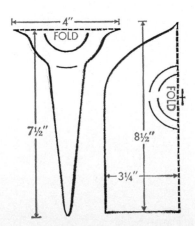

Stylized Star

Christmas Tree Forest

Personalized cards with the hand-crafted touch are remembered much longer than any others. Using the cards above as models, try creating your own. **Stylized Star** card begins with standard-size construction paper folded in half, then one half folds in half the other direction. Pink star is construction paper, red star is tissue. Gold foil star tops trio. **Christmas Tree Forest** card has white construction paper folded, cut as at left, glued to green paper, then topped by blue and green paper and sequins.

Children's sewing cards inspired these greeting cards. To copy, sketch designs on

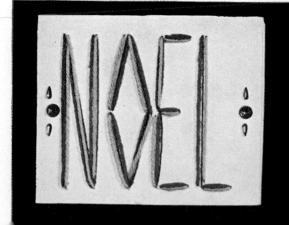

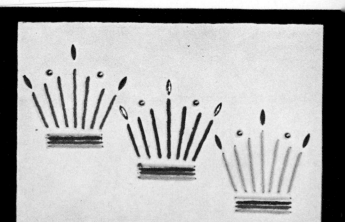

Yuletide Bell   **Pleated Tree**

Yuletide Bell card uses standard-size construction paper folded in half, then folded twice on each half at $1\frac{3}{4}$-inch and $3\frac{1}{2}$-inch intervals from ends. Make bell by cutting according to directions on the right. White paper adheres to red construction paper backing. Red tissue paper cutout glues to bell for interest. **Pleated Tree** card has tiers of accordion folded white paper glued to center fold of green construction paper. Yellow base folded and glued under tree and embossed gold star complete design.

cardboard; punch holes; lace yarn and secure in back. Add sequin and jewel accents.

GIFTS

Since that first Christmas over two thousand years ago when the three Wise Men from the East presented' their tokens of love to the Christ Child, Christmas has been a time of giving.

Gifts that are made by hand by the giver can be the most cherished and longest remembered. Among the gift suggestions that follow are ideas for simple objects for children to make for friends, ideas for constructive and recreational toys for adults to make for children, ideas for sewing creations for women to make for children and for other women, and even ideas for wood gifts for men to construct for the family.

Walnut stained toy chest was designed to use bits of leftover wood. To make the box, cut six plywood rectangles; two 26x22-inch pieces for front and back, two 20x22-inch pieces for sides, and two 20x26-inch pieces for top and bottom. Sand all edges smooth and nail together, fitting edges and corners neatly. Apply hinges so that lid may be open 270 degrees.

Applique one-inch-deep wood blocks and one-inch-wide by two-inch-deep wood strips on outside of box by gluing, then nailing with small nails. Use wood initial to personalize chest. Countersink nails for a more attractive finish. Complete chest by staining it walnut.

Friendly lion picture will delight both boys and girls. The lion is stitched to cotton ticking background that has been tightly stretched over a wood frame. The design was first sketched on paper, then transferred to the ticking with red pencil. Inexpensive wool rug yarn was used to create mane, tail, and beard loops of lion and body and spots of butterfly. Redraw on wrong side of material; fill in areas to be hooked using an automatic hooking needle.

Long running stitches form body of lion and grass. Lightweight black wool outlines the figure. And lightweight wool in a chain stitch creates the delightful butterfly.

Stylized Sandpipers on a 17½x39-inch burlap background playfully peck away on this wall hanging. Panel hangs from a wood dowel laced through burlap loops made by folding three-inch-long burlap bands in half.

Loops are fastened to panel with heavy-duty thread. A hem is stitched around all sides of burlap. Muslin lines loops and burlap panel. Birds are cut from burlap, then appliqued to backing with yarn. Beaks, legs, and butterfly are chain-stitched. Bird wings and tail are outlined with a couching stitch.

Cardboard community of prim little houses can grace table or base of a tree. Make each from 18x24-inch piece of lightweight art board. Fold board as in pattern above, and glue, attaching roofs separately. If desired, cut squares and rectangles for doors and windows; back with colored cellophane. Twirl lights around the village.

Empty jars and cans make clever banks for young savers. Cut slots in lids, being careful to remove sharp edges for safety. Then decorate with gay colors or designs. Discarded adhesive-strip boxes can be converted into safe storage for matches, fishhooks, and odds and ends. Paint boxes and let your children decorate them.

Framed Christmas keepsakes for every room in the house! Cut rounds of heavy cardboard and cover each with gift paper, fabric, bits of plastic. Then glue on toys, tree ornaments, a cherished card, or a small package exquisitely wrapped. Plaque at left is decorated with red plastic, small hand holding dolls, wired velvet tubing to finish. At right, the circle features striped fabric, tiny toy tree, and favorite greeting cards.

Young warriors will make many a conquest with these shields cut from 1/2-inch plywood. Apply crest of enamel or adhesive-backed plastic cutouts and fasten a leather strap on back. The swords are made of four pieces of scrap 3/8-inch plywood. Make the blade about two inches wide stepping down to one inch for the handle end. Cut a slot 3/8x1 inch in hand guard and slip up against blade. Glue small pieces on each side to form handle.

Magnificent treasure chest rescued from the attic holds children's dolls, toys, and gaily wrapped presents. If you do not have an old trunk to repaint and trim, then deck out a wooden crate or even a large cardboard box. Paint the outside or cover with paper. Attach commercially packaged Christmas designs and letters to the inside lid. After the holidays, the trunk can store decorations, children's toys, family games, or linens.

Cover favorite albums and scrapbooks with material, then sew, glue or iron on decorations. Cut the letters especially to personalize the album.

Keep Dad's maps together attractively in this easy-to-make map holder. You need just a single strip of felt, canvas, or heavy cotton long enough to form two pockets. Seal the edges with fabric cement or iron-on tape. Again, decorate with iron-on tape cutouts or fabric cutouts glued on to the billfold-type container. You can even put Dad's name or initials on the corner.

Counting board is easy-to-make of scrap fiberboard covered with felt. Pull the felt cover over the edge and glue, tack, or staple on the back. The numbers and corresponding number of figures are cut from colorful felt. It makes counting fun.

The story board is also a felt-covered fiberboard, made exactly the same as the counting board. You can start your child out by including a few ready-cut felt shapes. But also have several large pieces of felt handy so he can cut his own shapes and designs to tell a favorite rhyme or story.

Young people will enjoy making papier mache piggy banks for friends. Procedure is to inflate balloon, attach egg carton sections with masking tape to form nose and legs, half sections to form ears. Tear newspaper into strips, dip into water, cover balloon and egg carton sections. Add three more coats by dipping strips into a runny flour-and-water or wallpaper paste. Paper towel strips make even better strips for strong overcoating. Keep edges of paper smooth for a finished look. When the papier mache coats have dried, paint pig with shiny enamels. Pipe cleaner tails add to the "personality" of the pigs.

Yarn on burlap art makes colorful gifts for youngsters to give. Designs are traced lightly on burlap with pencil, applied with bobby pin needle. Felt appliques attached with white glue add interest. Designs may be made into placemats or wall hangings. Ideas can come from coloring books, or from imaginations.

Stoles above were knit on a hand-made loom. Loom measures 3¾ x 27½ inches and stands 4¼ inches tall. An uneven number (45) of No. 16 wire brads are spaced ½ inch apart across the loom with ½ inch distance between parallel nails. Brads also extend ½ inch above surface of loom. To thread, use methods A or B below, running the yarn over every other nail one way, then back over empty ones. Repeat process so there are two threads around each nail.

To knit, take up bottom thread with crochet hook. Pull loop over thread above it, drop on other side of nail. Repeat step at each nail. Each nail now has one thread. Set up threading pattern again. Add one row

to get stacked effect. Knit off bottom threads as before. Continue until stole is as long as desired. Beginning on loom right, pick up end stitch on one rail, drop over corresponding nail on opposite rail. Take lower thread, lift over upper thread and nail as in knitting. Repeat for each pair of nails. Begin again at right, take loop off first nail, drop next. Knit off one thread. Take remaining loop off nail, drop over third nail. Continue to last stitch, fasten as in regular knitting.

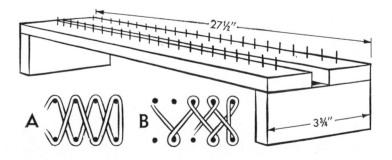

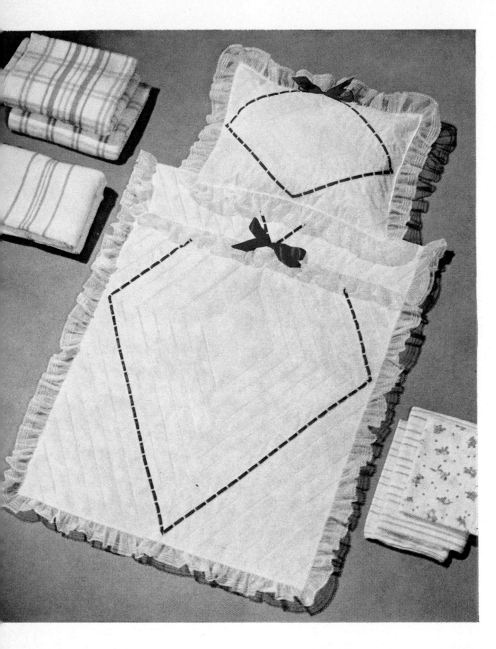

A carriage set for an infant makes a delightful and appreciated gift. Using two yards of organdy, cut two 24x36-inch pieces. Trim a receiving blanket to the same size. Using a yardstick, mark one layer of the nylon organdy in a diamond which nearly touches the center of each outside edge. Rule six diamonds inside the first, then lines out to the corners.

Pin the three thicknesses together (organdy and blanket). Stitch on lines, sewing first the center triangle and working out. Run ribbon (four yards of $\frac{1}{2}$-inch width) through five yards of nylon beading and stitch beading and ribbon to the outside diamond on the front side. Sew the remaining ribbon to the back on the same diamond covering just the front tip for six inches. When the blanket is turned down, this portion will be visible along the turned down edge.

Sew five yards of nylon ruffling around the outside edge, right sides together. Turn the ruffling out and stitch near edge of blanket. Fold the top edge down five inches; stitch the edges together and tack on a bow. Make a matching pillowcase from $12\frac{1}{2}$x$16\frac{1}{2}$ pieces of organdy and blanket, with back opening for pillow.

Any nondetailed A-line dress pattern would be flattered by accents of a petitely designed woven tape such as the one illustrated at the far left. And, if you choose a design with a natural neckline, the trimming pictured on the girl standing above can be easily reproduced.

When choosing dress pattern, fabric, and trim consider the size of the child and her coloring. Sew dress leaving the hem unfinished. Form a tailored bow of tape and hand-tack it to dress. Pin streamers in place and attach with hand stitching. Put in hem to complete dress.

Another basic A-line dress trimming idea is to form numbers at hemline as on dress worn by balloon-carrying Miss above. The neckline style will not matter for this idea, so choose your pattern and fabric to suit the time of year, the child's age, and the pattern or color to be used for trim.

Once again, make dress following directions in pattern. Leave neckline, sleeves, and hemline unfinished. Bind all three with double-fold bias tape in either matching or contrasting color. Now shape numbers with the bias tape. Cut, fold, or tuck angles. Applique figures in place.

Make a Christmas ruler for each child in the family. For hanging, cut white duck 16x55½ inches. Mark across width seven inches from the bottom, then mark every six inches six more times. Stitch middy braid across marks. Cut off tape measure at 11½ inches, fold under edge to 12-inch mark. Place it one inch from bottom and 9½ inches from left side; stitch to duck. Bind lengthwise edges with bias tape. Turn under one inch on both ends, then fold under ¼ inch, stitch across width forming casing. Cut holly leaves, berries from iron-on tape. Iron on across top. Insert wood dowel rods through casings, hang ruler 12 inches from floor.

Sewing trims, available in multitudes at notion counters across the country, can help you give your little girl dresses finished with the look of professional designing.

The empire waistline dress adapts itself readily for a truly delightful design for a little girl's best dress. Here is one style suggestion to try, but there is no end to the variation possibilities. Select a simple empire style pattern and a pretty fabric, then find the "just right" trim from the notions counter. This crisp white eyelet ruffling goes well with almost any cotton fabric, patterned or plain.

Follow the directions in the pattern. When the dress is completed, add row after row of fluffy white eyelet strips as drawing on the left suggests. Be sure to allow a bit of an overlap to achieve a full effect. Finish designer touch with colorful ribbon band at the top and a matching bow at the back and for her hair.

HOW TO CHOOSE TOYS The cherished wooden wagon a father once made for his son, or the doll clothes a mother made to match a dress of her own, conveyed love to their children and made them aware that they were special people.

A child feels joy and pride in receiving a toy designed for him. It is especially his own. There is joy, too, for the creator of such a unique gift, for he is giving more than the made-to-order toy. He is giving part of himself, his thoughts, his hands, his time. These are the greatest and most precious gifts that man has to give. To share these gifts with a child through a toy made "just for him" is sharing something nobody else can give. It is personal, unique, and his to give.

A toy should be more than a momentary diversion. A toy can help a child acquire the value of the culture in which he is growing. A toy can arouse curiosity; create challenge; stimulate imagination and creativity. A toy can hasten learning, aid concentration, and provide the fun of doing, also develop interests and skills. Most of all, however, it can give experience. A toy offers fantasy. A toy belongs securely in the world of the child. By giving a child the right toy, you provide him with a tool for learning what you want him to learn, to value what you value.

Planning the right toy means that you consider what children, in general, are like, what a particular child's interests and abilities are, and how and why children play as they do. Most children, for example, are active and noisy. Playing with toys provides a way and a time to be "legitimately" so.

Sometimes children are quiet and need to play alone. Other times they want comrades in their play. They need toys that will provide and encourage both play forms. Many toys can fill this dual requirement.

During quiet and active play times, children's needs vary from toys that offer a challenge to their minds to toys that let them "mess around" with no purpose except to have the fun of doing something. The fascination of a mechanical toy may wane when the battery wears out, causing the passive participant to become active in asking for it to be repaired, or to have a new one. Conversely, a toy that leaves the inner functionings to a child's imagination will generally hold the child's attention far longer.

Well-chosen toys are ones that suit a particular child's interests and abilities. They are ones that stimulate him to do something, rather than passively watch. Well-chosen toys can develop a child's skills and resourcefulness, his imagination, and creativeness. They may develop the potential which is in each child to become the person he has the potential of becoming. Through toys children may discover and experience a great deal about the world, about themselves, and about some of their problems, as well as about some of the wonders and joys of life.

Boxes, boards, and ladders may be arranged in an infinite variety of positions to be used by one child or many. They will last for years and the cost of making them in quality wood will be more than offset by greater safety and longer wear. Pieces may be designed to suit the needs of your children, or there are patterns available commercially or from state universities.

Ages 3 to 10

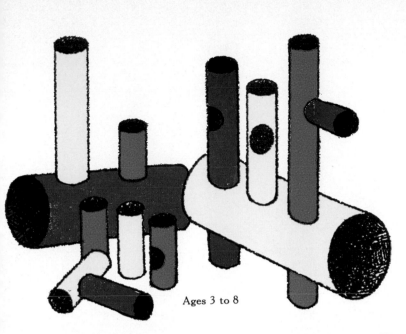

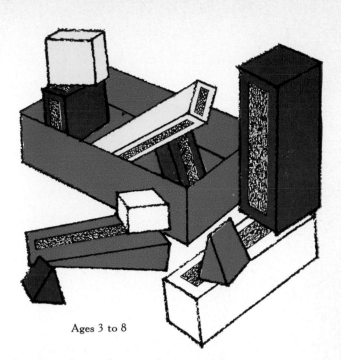

Ages 3 to 8

Ages 3 to 8

Cardboard cylinders make a mix-matching game of special interest and appeal to children of all ages. To insure accurate fit, diameters are measured for each role used, then any number of holes designed are cut in each one. Before the holes are cut, the cylinders are spray-painted in different colors, or are covered with self-adhesive, colorful, vinyl plastic.

Intricate interlocking of these plywood pieces is made possible by careful cutting of slits, and equally careful sanding, painting, and finishing. Blocks require strength and well-developed eye-hand coordination generally found in children in kindergarten or first grade. Challenge and appeal of structures that can be made may extend to still older children.

Enamel-painted wooden blocks in a variety of sizes, shapes, and assorted colors attract children of almost any age. To each of these blocks a strip of nylon tape fastener has been glued, making blocks put-together-take-apart construction toys, rather than the usual building materials. Blocks might be made without the nylon tape and still provide a plaything.

Squares, triangles, and rectangles cut from wood scraps combine in futuristic designs. Pieces have holes drilled partially through them in each corner and on sides. All are spray-painted with enamel. Combined with wood dowels of different lengths, blocks can be put together in multi-angular and various-sized structures. Perforated cardboard strip serves as foundation.

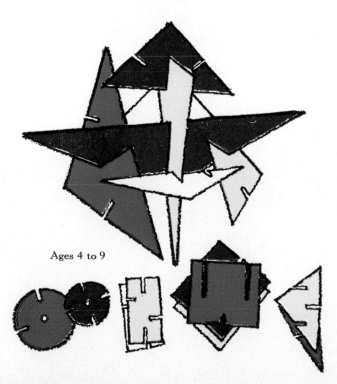

Ages 4 to 9

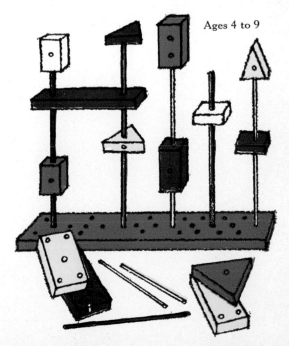

Ages 4 to 9

Ages 2 to 3

Ages 2 to 5

Hide-and-find toy can be made inexpensively of a large cereal box with holes cut in lid and wooden pieces cut to match each hole. This one has wooden lid mounted on three pegs that fit inside box when lid is on, and that make the lid stand two inches off the floor when it is removed from the box.

Zip! Button! Snap! A child at the "let-me-do-it!" stage will delight in practicing, in doing over and over, these engaging skills. Shape or expression of fabric face should be varied by fastener arrangements.

Wooden train has engine and box cars with tops that open. Tops have holes for wood and metal washer cargo. Cars and cargo are painted in primary-color enamels.

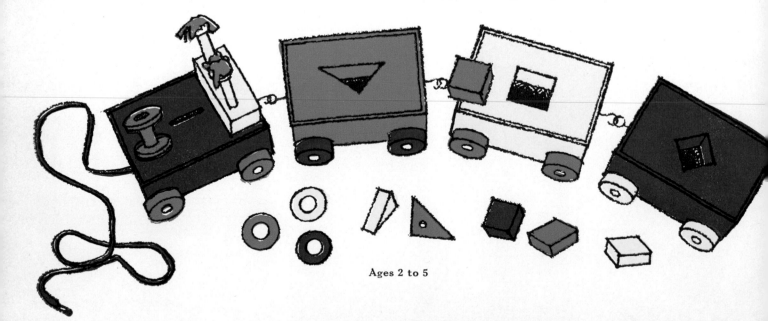

Ages 2 to 5

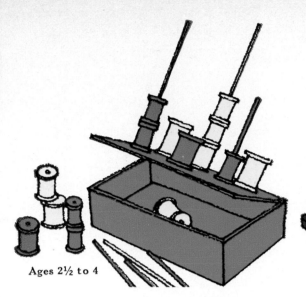

Ages 2½ to 4

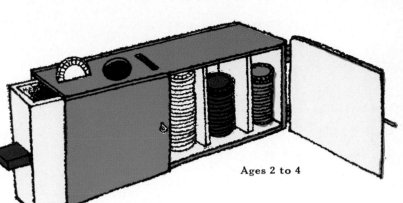

Ages 2 to 4

Spools and cigar box game is for learning to match colors and sizes, also for developing eye-hand coordination in stacking. Cigar box stores spools and dowels. Spool of each size and color is glued to box lid, then dowel may be put in spool and other spools laced over it.

Poker chip drop box, upper right, provides three ways for a child to drop chips into pull-out drawer, also a place to store chips when not in use. Game offers opportunity to learn discrimination of shape and color; also provides repetition, a part of early learning.

Bell-tailed turtle is going places! It jingles along on four spool feet as it is pulled by a young walker. Balsa wood body is enamel painted. Spool head is topped by rubber chair tip which has an expressive face created by dotting it with enamel paint eyes.

Criteria for Choosing Toys

1. Consider the child: Watch what he does, what his particular interests and abilities are, and what further interests might be encouraged.

2. Consider the toy: What can the child do with it? What purpose or purposes has it? What does it tell the child about what you value and want him to learn? How long will the toy last? How much space is needed to use it and to store it?

3. Consider the construction: Is material suitable for its use, safe, smoothly finished? Is paint nontoxic? Is toy simple and uncluttered in line and design? Will the toy work as intended for its lifetime?

4. Consider the cost: Is it in relation to length of life of toy and purposes to which it may be put?

5. Consider a "balanced diet" of toys: It should be balanced in kind to include some for active, some for quiet, play; and some for using the whole body; also, some for using one or another particular part of the body. Others should be for playing alone and some should be for sharing with friends. Some should set a definite task to be accomplished, while some should let the child be what and who he needs to be.

Ages 1 to 2

Get ready for your Christmas guests early this year by making these gay, red accessories for the family's party apparel. The easy-to-make designs of corduroy, felt, and organdy can repeat the colors of your yuletide decorations.

The red corduroy vest will fit most sizes with a little modification. The vest has only two basic pieces stitched together at the neck as shown in the top pattern at the right.

To make the vest, place the pattern on corduroy folded with nap on outside, cut around pattern, mark button and buttonhole spots. Bind all edges of the vest and pocket with black bias tape, extending tape on both sides at arrow to make ties to fit across back. Fit the vest to the future wearer, if possible, marking where neck tabs should overlap and pockets should lie for good style. Machine-stitch neck tabs together and make the pocket, shaping pockets according to pattern. Add buttonholes and buttons.

Christmas bib of corduroy for a doll or new baby has bright red cotton lining and a white felt tree design. To copy the bib, place shoulder line of pattern at right on fold of corduroy with nap running the length of the bib. For back opening, cut bib down center as indicated. Line the corduroy with red cotton, adding corduroy tabs under arms connecting front of apron to the back. Decorate felt tree with sequins, outline with rickrack, and hand-tack to the apron.

The red organdy apron on the little girl begins with a red rectangle folded up twice as indicated in the pattern at right and pressed in place. Next white fringe is stitched along the hem and the side edges are folded under and secured with folded edge on front side. Double rows of stitching make the pockets across bottom of apron. Complete apron with two-inch-wide belt attached to apron top with six darts across the top. Add green felt and silver bells.

Red vest for the younger "man" of the family can be made in minutes and at very little cost. To copy, fold felt in half, cut two front pieces as pattern on right indicates. Next, place center back piece on fold of felt, cut around pattern. Hand- or machine-stitch side seams of front and back pieces together, then the shoulders. Use a single-edged razor blade to slit four buttonholes. Sew on bell buttons positioned corresponding to slits. Cut white felt key and watch face, black felt watch back. Attach tiny red beads to watch face for numbers, embroider black hands. Hand-tack watch and key to vest.

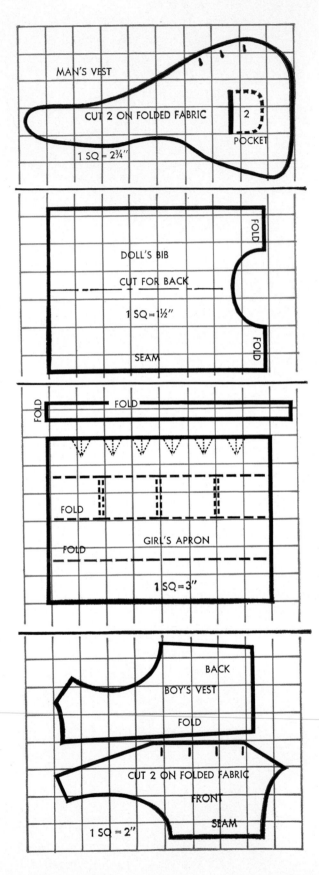

Make him a tie: Imported wools, decorator and designer silks offer excellent materials for you to create handsome ties with the look of a professional touch. Imagine how proud the man who receives one of your ties will be to wear it, as he receives enthusiastic compliment after compliment from his friends!

When selecting choice tie fabrics, consider tie silk or fine woolens. The expense is so nominal you can easily afford the finest imports. Keep textures and colors simple, subtle if you have any doubt as to what is "in" for the season. Or let your color sense go wild!

To make a tie, you must first decide whether it will have a V-bottom or square-bottom. In the directions that follow, use the figures or words in parentheses for V-bottom ties, main figures for square-bottom ties.

You will need 54 inches for the length of the tie. By cutting across the fabric, 4 (4½) inches will be sufficient for the width. If the material is less than 54 inches wide, buy two widths or 8 (9) inches; cut material in half crosswise, and machine-stitch one end of each together. If the tie has a pattern, match the sections as closely as possible. Press seam open neatly.

Draw a tie on thin cardboard salvaged from the sheets inserted in shirts at the laundry or from a dress box. Use a ready-made tie for your pattern. Several strips will be needed to cover the 54-inch length. Cut around pieces and number them in sequence. These will serve in directions as forms.

Make a tie pattern from wrapping paper or an opened grocery sack. Place the cardboard forms in sequence on the paper. Starting at the widest end, the width of the tie form will measure about 1½ (2) inches. To establish the width of the pattern, double the form width and add one inch. Divide these 4 (5) inches on either side of the form center, making outside margins of 1¼ (1½) inches. Mark outside edges of margins. Continue measuring, marking up entire length of tie, then join marks together with a continuous line. Cut along the line and attach pieces together with cellophane tape, if the pattern has been cut in several sections.

Line 1½ inch of wide end of tie with silk or rayon in a dark color. With right sides facing, stitch a narrow seam at bottom. Pass open flat, then turn lining to underside and press in place. Open lining flat again and center first section of form on right side of material. Draw

sides firmly, not tightly, over form. Pin together up center from tip of lining to about one inch into tie fabric. Remove form, machine-stitch where pinned. Turn lining inside.

(Cut about 6 inches on lining and pin to tie fabric, right sides together. Center V'd tip of form about ½ inch from edge. Outline V with chalk, extending lines out to edge of fabric. (See drawing.) Machine-stitch side 1 along line from tip to side edge. Trim seam to ¼ inch. Evenly fold this entire seam forward ½ inch and pin. Stitch over this fold at side edge and down side 3 about ¼ inch from edge. Stitch over fold at tip and down side 2. Trim seam, fold lower end of side 2 forward the same way. Stitch over end of fold and down side 4. Turn and press. Lining will be set in from edge.)

Unstitch an outdated tie and remove the tie "filler" material. Use the cardboard forms as a guide and cut the filler slightly narrower than the cardboard. The length of the filler is usually shorter than the tie.

Insert first form into finished end of tie. Center short seam over form beginning where lining ends. (Insert filler, cut to V, to top of point and pin.) Slide a narrow cardboard to top between filler and tie fabric. Baste filler loosely to center of lining and far enough up from tip to be hidden when sides are folded in. Remove cardboard. Cut filler at end of lining. Match tip of form with tip of tie and center forms up length of tie material. Place tie filler on forms beginning where lining ends.

Fold margin at one side of form flat over form. Hold down and wrap opposite margin across and overlap the first. Fold under last margin about ¼ inch so folded edge will fall up center of tie, catching the filler every few inches.

With forms still in place, steam press tie on seamed side. The cardboard will keep the seam from standing up on right side of tie after pressing. Remove all forms from wide end except the narrowest strip. This one will be more convenient to the other opening. Fold in raw edge ¼ inch at narrow end. Slip-stitch together. If the edges of the tie aren't sharp enough after removing the cardboard, wipe brown wrapping paper with a damp cloth and steam press the tie lightly. The seam line will not be visible on the top side.

The creative man can help at Christmas by making some of the gifts, too. If the family likes to collect mementos from vacation trips, let him present to the rest of the household a permanent scrapbook of family adventures. The handsome sand collage at the left combines white sand from the Utah desert; black sand from Montserrat, British West Indies; gray sand from the Sacramento River bed; driftwood from Folsom and Cascade Lakes in California and from Antigua, British West Indies; and kelp roots from the Washington State coastal areas.

First outline a pattern on a plywood rectangle. Next, brush each area separately with white liquid glue and a coat of sand. Secure all materials (except sea urchins, starfish) with wood screws. Attach starfish with glue to a flathead screw which is screwed into the plywood at the desired location.

Finally, spray a second and larger plywood rectangle with flat black paint and use for the backing. Use small, level, wood blocks to raise collage one inch above black frame. Secure frame, blocks, and collage backing with long wood screws in back.

Map-covered file for Dad to keep maps in one place and a pattern file for Mother are made from about-to-be-discarded cartons. Cotton-covered pattern file has paper tape measure and newspaper letters glued on; maps letters come from a magazine.

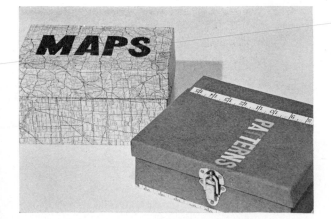

Twine and wood frame structure, below, can lend itself to a variety of decorating uses. Pine frame of 1x3s measures 41x54 inches. One-inch nails pound partially into front of frame at ½-inch intervals. Spring twine loops at one end, hooks over a nail in upper corner, runs diagonally down frame to wrap around another nail.

Next, it travels back same route to wrap around a nearby nail, runs back down at a diagonal to a corresponding nail. Wrapping continues until design is completed, then twine ties on last nail. Strips of corner bead nail to frame hiding nails. Walnut stain, varnish finish frame.

The handsome checkerboard table (above) doubles as a game and as an end table and is another project for the man of the house. The tabletop measures 24 inches square and the entire table stands 22 inches high. The board may also be used without legs or may be stored in the closet. The table can be made and assembled using only hand tools. The top is formed of ¾ inch thick plywood covered by 3x3-inch-cork tapered edge squares cut from three 12-inch square cork tiles purchased at a floor tile store.

Screw-in legs and half of the squares were stained to desired finish before use. Squares should be dark enough to give good contrast for checker playing and subtle enough for pleasing use as an extra piece of furniture in the family room.

The cork is glued to the plywood with white liquid glue, taking care to fit the tiles well to insure a professional look. Walnut stripping around the edges covers the corking area. The checkers are cut from a 24-inch long and 1½-inch in diameter wood dowel. Half are stained with the dark walnut finish and half are varnished for the light color.

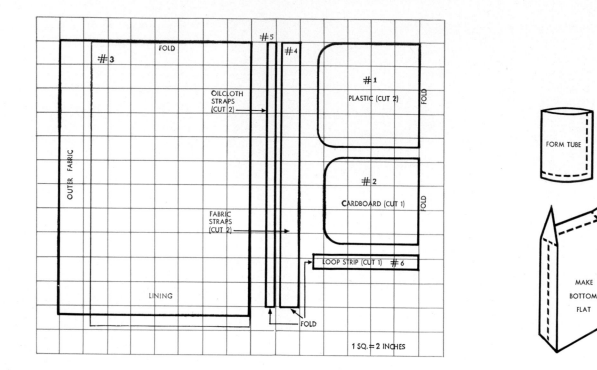

To reproduce plastic-lined, striped tote bag, center heavy cardboard base (2) between two plastic pieces (1), right sides out. Pin around edge, stretch tightly. Lay base on tissue paper for sewing (plastic cannot feed through machine). With zipper foot, stitch closely around cardboard edges. Remove tissue paper.

Stitch lining sides together. Stitch outer fabric, right sides together. Press, turn right side out. Lay flat, seam at one side. Mark on lower edge of fabric $6\frac{1}{4}$ and $14\frac{1}{4}$ inches from seam (strap attachments). Measure down from top edge $4\frac{1}{4}$ inches, mark same as bottom for loops.

Center oilcloth (5) on wrong side of fabric (4). Fold fabric over oilcloth and press edges lengthwise. Turn under raw edges of fabric until $\frac{1}{4}$ inch remains along side. Pin in place; machine-stitch close to center edge on both sides.

Fold material loop (6) in thirds the length of the strip. Press. Double under half of last third; stitch along edge. (Stitching will be down center of loop.) Cut strip into four parts. Double ends under so flattened loops measure $1\frac{1}{2}$ inches. Hand-stitch to hold. Center loops on marks at top edge of bag; hand-stitch ends of underneath side of loops to bag. Thread straps through.

With wrong side out, pin right edge of lining to seam allowance of base. (Center side seam at middle of base end.) Turn base over. With wrong side of fabric out, pin right lower edge to base. Base seam allowances are now between right side

edges of lining and fabric. Slip strap ends through at marks. Pin in place between fabric and base. With zipper foot, stitch through all layers as close to cardboard as possible.

Finish bag by turning outer fabric right side out, stretching up taut along with straps. Hand-stitch straps to fabric through back of loop. Pin lining near top. Fold fabric over top of lining. Turn under raw edge of fabric one inch, pin. Machine-stitch close to edge on inside.

Black and brown bag is made by folding in half one each 36x13-inch pieces of black and brown burlap; seaming sides; folding down, fringing edges, and adding black straps.

To copy pink lined bag, cut burlap and lining pieces $22\frac{1}{2}$x$15\frac{1}{2}$ inches. Fold burlap over; stitch short sides together. Stitch bottom edges together; press seams. Flatten bottom section with bottom seam centered; stitch 3-inch seam at each corner. Trim off triangle extensions above seam. Turn inside out. Make lining similarly.

Place 3x$6\frac{1}{2}$-inch cardboard in bottom of bag. Cut burlap piece $6\frac{1}{2}$x12 inches for pocket. Stitch around piece $\frac{1}{2}$ inch from edge. Fringe edges. Sew to front of bag leaving top open. Insert lining topstitch to burlap bag at top edges; catch $1\frac{1}{2}$x13 inch lined straps at either side. Decorate pockets. For interchangeable side panels, use snaps to attach panels to sides.

Coral embroidered apron

Embroidered blue apron

Royal blue apron begins with a 38½-inch-wide, 28-inch-long piece of cotton broadcloth. The rectangle has 1½-inch-wide hems turned back on the sides, then the top of apron gathers to fit and attaches to the tapered waistband. Before ends of waistband are secured, 26-inch-long hemmed ties are inserted. Next, side hems and a three-inch lower hem are stitched.

Finally, embroidery stitches are added for decoration. The Feather Stitch borders waistband and ties, the skirt, and the pockets. A Chain Stitch waves along ties, across waistband, and on pockets, also forms the outline for flowers and leaves. Yellow French Knots add accent.

Coral-colored apron with floral petite design begins with a 36-inch-wide and 19½-inch-long rectangle of cotton. The selvages are used for the sides of the apron and the bottom has a three-inch-wide hemline. The top is gathered and attached to a 15-inch-long waistband. The ties, 23 inches in length, attach to the ends of the waistband and are hemmed by hand.

Royal blue Feather Stitching borders ties and waistband, skirt, and pockets. It also connects the dainty flowers running across the waistband and creates stems for the flowers on pocket, hem, and tie ends. Eight petal flowers formed by a Lazy-daisy Stitch and French Knots add detail.